Secret Encounters

For my parents.
Thanks for the good upbringing
and the good genes.
—*Michael Shelton*

Secret Encounters

Addressing Sexual Behaviors in Group Settings

Michael Shelton, M.S., C.A.C., C.F.T.

The issues addressed in this book are sensitive and even potentially volatile. Response to these issues is highly personal. We, the author and publisher, hope that this book will help you consider the issues around sexual behaviors in a group setting. Rather than advocating a single response, the book is intended to generate the thought and dialog necessary to help readers develop a plan for addressing these behaviors suited to the camp's environment, mission, and beliefs.

This material is sold with the understanding that the author, Michael Shelton, and the publisher, American Camping Association, are not engaged in rendering legal, psychological, medical, or other professional services. If legal, psychological, medical, or other expert assistance is required, the services of a competent professional should be sought.

Special thanks are given to photographer James T. Hurne of Westminster Highlands Camp, Emlenton, Pennsylvania, for the use of this fine collection of photographs depicting the very best of camp—the fun, the friendships, and the enriching of lives through camp experiences!

Cover design by Joyce Koeper
Text edited and designed by The Versatile Wordsmith

We invite your comments on this book. Please write to the American Camping Association at the address or e-mail below.

American Camping Association, Inc.
5000 State Road 67 North
Martinsville, Indiana 46151-7902
765-342-8456 National Office
800-428-2267 Bookstore
www.ACAcamps.org
bookstore@ACAcamps.org

A CIP catalog record for this book can be obtained from the Library of Congress.

Contents

*Somewhere between overzealous oversight
and head-in-the-sand denial of sexual
behavior lies a middle ground.*

Introduction

Not long ago, I was responsible for hiring male staff members at a residential camp. A number of staff from the previous season had already informed me that they would be returning. One of them was 19-year-old Wayne. In our telephone contact, Wayne said he didn't want to be a counselor like last summer. He really wanted to be a unit leader. I had to tell him he simply wasn't old enough to be a unit leader. What I didn't tell Wayne was that some of his judgments last summer had been questionable. Nothing serious had occurred, but he clearly lacked the maturity for a supervisory position. I had decided that Wayne needed several more years of camp experience to "grow" into the unit leader position, but I was happy to hire him again as a counselor.

Two weeks later, Wayne's application and supporting documents arrived in the mail. I figured this meant one less position to fill now that Wayne was on board. As the summer season approached, I phoned Wayne several times. Nobody answered. I left messages on an answering machine. None were returned.

The last thing I needed during this busy the month before camp was to waste time on non-responsive staff. But, despite Wayne's immaturity, he had added to the camp environment last season, and I wanted him back. I searched through the pile of staff medical forms on my desk and found Wayne's. His emergency contact was listed as his grandmother, so I called her. She told me Wayne would not be able to be come to camp this summer. When I asked why, she vaguely responded that "something else had come up." So that season, we had to do without Wayne.

This would be the end of the story, except that Wayne and I did meet again in what became a very uncomfortable situation for both of us.

A year later, as part of my graduate internship, I was placed at the Joseph J. Peters Institute in Philadelphia. The Institute is renowned throughout the country for its treatment of sexual offenders and victims of sexual abuse, and this internship matched nicely with my clinical experience in behavioral disorders. It was there that I again encountered Wayne. We saw each other as he was stepping off of the elevator. Before I could even acknowledge him, he stepped back into the elevator. When he discovered, through his therapist, that I was an intern at the Institute, he made sure his schedule would never again match mine, thus avoiding any accidental contact.

I later learned that Wayne had been arrested several weeks before the start of the aforementioned camp season for child molestation. He had reportedly fondled two female children who lived in his neighborhood. He had completed more than a year of residential placement and was now in a six-month outpatient program at the Institute.

This news wracked me with concern. How could I have hired a "child molester" and, even worse, almost hired him back? Could he have had sexual contact with any children at camp? Though the boys' and girls' camps were run independently, they did have frequent contact. How could I have been so blind?

Looking back on that summer, I realized I wasn't blind—there really was nothing to see. Wayne had good references. His clearances indicated no experience with the legal system or any charge of offending against children. Nobody at camp complained about inappropriate sexual behavior on his part. Wayne had acted immaturely on occasion, but overall he had been a dependable employee and an asset to the camp spirit. Incidentally, a polygraph test taken at the Institute revealed that Wayne's only victims were the two girls in his neighborhood.

This incident alerted me to the reality that teenagers are perpetrators in a large number of sexual offenses. I thought this was important enough to warrant an article in the American Camping Association's *Camping Magazine*. I had already written a number of well-received articles for ACA and expected that this latest article on the possible effects of teenage sexual offending in camps would likewise be appreciated. The magazine's editor surprised me by saying that, though she agreed the article was important, she would not print it unless I inserted "easy solutions" for readers. I refused, because easy solutions do not exist. To suggest they did would have been a disservice to readers. Obviously, the time was not yet right to share this information.

In the years since then, I have grown used to discussing sex and sexual concerns on a daily basis in a clinical setting. Naturally, this ease with the subject has transferred to my consulting with camp directors. Though my consulting focuses on leadership, supervision, and organizational development, once the directors learn of my clinical work, they ask pertinent questions about sexual behaviors that have occurred in their camps. Sometimes they even ask about sexual behaviors in which they themselves actually or almost participated. Or, they ask about poor judgments they made largely due to sexual arousal, being only human and experiencing the same sexual urges as people everywhere.

Just as my clinical and camp work has converged on issues of sexuality, sexual behavior at camps has become a "hot issue" in the camp community. Camp conferences now offer workshops and trainings, and more and more camp directors contact me specifically about sexual issues in their camps.

Although pleased that the camp community is acknowledging the existence of sexual behavior in the camp setting, I think much of the concern is misplaced. Camps appear to be following the same path that day care centers and schools have taken, labeling all sexual behaviors as problematic or even dangerous. Tobin (1997) paints a rather stark picture of our collective approach:

> In their responses to masturbating, kissing, and playing-doctor scenarios, we have seen Americans dealing with children's sexual play by calling for medical or child abuse consultations…. The introduction into preschools of tools and perspectives borrowed from the medical doctor, the psychiatrist, the social worker, the policeman, the lawyer, and the insurance agent works to further disempower rather than protect teachers and children…(p. 147).

Activities that were once innocuous and age-appropriate have suddenly become problematic. Thinking back to my days as a camp counselor more than decade ago, I wonder if the activities that occurred then would now be considered objectionable. For example, I once worked with a group of eight-year-old boys. We would hike to a pond some distance from the camp and swim in our underwear. Would this be forbidden now? Or how about hugging the boys in my cabin good night? This was a custom in the unit for the youngest children. My guess is that now we would receive negative feedback about this contact.

I am confident, though, that a rational way can be found to approach sex and sexuality in camps. **Somewhere between overzealous oversight and head-in-the-sand denial of all sexual behavior lies a middle ground for camp directors.**

With this book, I have set out to accomplish four ambitious goals. By the time you finish reading it, I hope you will have the knowledge and tools to:

- Understand how personal values and beliefs influence people's reactions to sex and sexuality in camps.

- Create a camp environment and culture less conducive to inappropriate sexual behavior.

- Distinguish between appropriate and inappropriate sexual behavior.

- Respond to appropriate and inappropriate sexual events when they occur.

Chapter 1 challenges you to question your own knowledge of human sexuality. It ends with several exercises to evaluate personal opinions, values, and knowledge of sex and sexuality. It is not uncommon for people to have conflicting values in many spheres of life. You need to understand how any confusion, lack of clarity, ambivalence, and/or conflict in your own values may affect the way you incorporate the material of this book into your life and your camp.

Chapters 2 and 3 take on the goal of creating a psychologically and physically safe camp environment. They address misconceptions about sex and camps that keep people from intervening proactively to avoid problems. They present the latest research on antisocial behavior in organizations and methods to reduce their occurrence. They also address the difficulty of gathering accurate information about sexual behaviors.

Chapters 4 through 7 cover four areas where sexual problems are likely to occur in a camp setting: sexual assault, sexual harassment, childhood sexuality, and child sexual abuse. Although the list of sexual crimes and psychological sexual disorders is quite long, most do not naturally occur in a camp setting. One would not expect a serial rapist at a camp, for example, nor would one expect obscene phone calls. We have concentrated on those areas where most problem sexual behaviors are encountered in camps.

A final chapter focuses on interventions for the camp director against inappropriate sexual behavior. In comparison to Chapter 3, which describes general interventions to combat antisocial activity, Chapter 8 looks at interventions geared to counteract sexual activity and lessen its harmful impacts. Repeating my earlier concern, you should know that no "one size fits all" solution exists. You will need to think through the information carefully to apply it successfully to your camp.

Many of you reading this book are well aware of the sexual episodes that occur at camp. Others wonder if this is really such a big deal, believing that their polices and methods of enforcement are enough to prevent inappropriate sexual behavior. My experience says sexual behavior at camp must be taken seriously. Though the great majority of sexual activity is harmless, it takes only a single negative event to destroy a camp's reputation.

I hope you find this book to be the beginning of an enlightening and helpful journey.

*Sex and sexuality are viewed through
a lens of personal feelings, values,
and attitudes.*

The

Ask yourself a fundam
Should be an easy yes or no, r
next few pages.

At a conference worksh
people to discuss this same q
camps were in attendance, I pu   ...e groups. After fifteen
minutes, we reconvened to shar   ...ponses.

The results were intriguing to say the least. Not one person denied the presence of sex in camps—in fact, there was a unanimous acceptance of this. But whether sex was a problem was by no means agreed upon. Some administrative staff claimed there was no problem with sex in camps, while the line staff of these same camps claimed quite the opposite. In other cases staff opinions were reversed: Line staff held sexual intimacies harmless, while administrators cited dangerous repercussions.

Who was right? Just when is sexual behavior in camp a "problem"? Is it when a complaint is lodged? When sexual behavior affects job performance? When it goes against the moral beliefs of the camp administration? Is it only a problem if the people involved are caught? A clear case of child molestation or rape leaves little doubt that it is both wrong and illegal, but fortunately such crimes are rare in camps.

As you read this book, consider this: **Most sexual activity occurring in camps is not illegal but morally and ethically vague.** Consequently, people in the camp field do not have a clear answer to "Is sexual behavior a problem in camps?" The question is open to disagreement, misunderstanding, and sometimes even ill will.

If the topic of sexuality is inherently ambiguous, how does a camp director decide what is appropriate and allowable in his or her camp? An example illustrates the challenge in formulating a policy on sexual behavior.

I attended a board meeting as part of my coaching agreement with a seasoned camp director. The prior summer, a staff member had been terminated for inappropriate sexual behavior with another staff member. The board of directors wanted a briefing on how to minimize such episodes in future camp seasons. As I watched the six assembled

...h had his or her own belief about ...d toward a more permissive approach, ...long as it didn't interfere with job respon- ...pt unaware of the relations. The most vocal ...site view. To her, any sexual activity in camp was ...tween campers was sufficient to send them both ...mance or sex to occur in camp. Other members of the ...somewhere along the continuum. Again, who was right?

...enters the field with a "blank slate" in regard to sex and sexu- ...racter traits, our parents' values and behaviors, our spiritual and ...ds, our peers, our own dating and sexual experiences, and the overall ...up in—all these affect our perspective. A camp director used to numer- ...sexual liaisons may have a vastly different view of what constitutes accept- ...al behaviors than a director who refrained from having sex until entering a ...itted relationship. You, too, come to the topic of sex and sexuality holding a num- ...r of beliefs about what is appropriate and inappropriate behavior. These beliefs will play no small part in the policies that you set for your camp.

No "Official" Policy

Because of the ambiguity surrounding sex and sexuality, we cannot expect our leaders in the camping industry to formulate an official policy. Although standards and guidelines exist for almost all other areas of camp life, there is as yet no consensus on sexual behavior. No camp director would allow a child to swim in a pool unattended, and would call a colleague negligent who allowed this. Yet whether to offer condoms to staff members through the infirmary, as some camps do, is subject to heated argument.

The camping industry seems to agree upon only four guidelines with regard to sex:

1. Never be alone with a child.

2. Exercise caution in physical contact with a child.

3. Staff should refrain from engaging in discussions of their personal lives with campers, especially the sexual aspects.

4. Have a sexual harassment policy in place.

Not all camps succeed in carrying out all four practices. Most probably follow the first three guidelines, but far fewer manage to establish a sexual harassment policy.

While helpful in some situations, the four guidelines cannot be generalized to numerous other sexual activities. Consider two same-aged campers who willingly engage in sexual intercourse. Or consider the staff member caught masturbating in the forest by several campers on a nature hike. How should a director respond? Because consensus is lacking, each camp is likely to respond in its own way. When I present the latter example (an actual case) at conference sessions, the varied responses from camp professionals indicate this very lack of consensus.

Lacking accord on what constitutes appropriate and inappropriate sexual activity, most directors rely on their own judgment. When sexual encounters occur, a director must make two primary judgments:

- Is the sexual activity inappropriate?

- If so, how do I respond?

But on what can the director base this judgment? With few guidelines available, and usually little time or interest in researching the topic, most directors rely on their internal bearings to guide them to a decision. Despite the best of intentions, their internal bearings may lead them to make mistakes.

Directors may formulate a judgment based on a personal value system that is contrary to what is expected, appropriate, and even healthy sexual activity. In anything other than clear-cut cases of illegal behavior, this can be problematic.

We all have sexual beliefs and values, but we rarely consider how we developed such beliefs or whether they are based on accurate information. Yet these insights are essential if a camp director is to make a well thought out decision when sexual activity is discovered.

The camp director's quest to form well-considered judgments regarding sexual activity encounters two obstacles.

- We are inundated with mixed messages about sex in our lives.

- Most people have a poor understanding of human sexuality.

We'll look at both of these factors in this chapter as we examine the inherent problems we encounter in forming our values about sex.

But first, a note of warning. To paraphrase an old adage, the closer something is, the more complicated it appears. A table is simply a table to a casual observer, yet quantum physics recognizes it as a swarm of interconnected particles. The latter understanding is far more complex. The same holds true for sex. The more one learns about it, the more difficult it becomes to view sexual behaviors as simply right or wrong. Even the middle ground between the extremes is precariously complicated.

This book will give you the more comprehensive understanding that you need, but this understanding may make decisions about sex and sexuality in camps more complicated. You have heard that with knowledge comes power. With such power also comes the need for more responsible decision making. Though increased knowledge may make your decisions more complex and time-consuming, this material will enable you to make more informed decisions about your camp and its policies on sexual behavior.

Mixed Messages

An extraterrestrial visitor observing sex in our culture would probably give up in confusion. We display a puzzling way of dealing with sex—endlessly fascinated with it, but acting as if it were morally wrong. People spend billions on pornography, but schools restrict sex education to an abstinence-based curriculum. Parents shy away from discussing sex with their children, while those same children daily watch near-pornographic music videos. The public finds fascinating the sexual exploits of the rich and famous, but those exploits ruin careers and reputations.

A battle is being waged between permissive and restrictive approaches to sex. The permissive stance views sex as pleasurable and healthy and part of a full and satisfying life. The restrictive stance views sex as dangerous and unhealthy and seeks to impose strict legal and social controls.

The last several generations have felt an increasing tension between these opposite poles. A child today sees advertisements on TV that would have shocked our grandparents with their sexual candor. Yet the same child is told by elders that sex is dangerous and for adults only. No wonder that your staff, campers, and possibly yourself hold conflicting views of sex. We are sexual beings who are told to restrain our sexuality. Is such restraint bad? Of course not. Is restraint sometimes difficult and confusing? Certainly.

Just as pornography is readily available but society sends the message that looking at it is "dirty," the tension between permissive and restrictive approaches results in mixed messages. Mixed messages lead to problems. One camp director informed staff that sexual activity on camp premises was forbidden and, if discovered, would result in termination, yet he had the nursing staff distribute condoms to staff who requested them. What were the staff to think? Don't be surprised if you recognize, as you read this book, that you've been an unknowing recipient of sexual mixed messages. You may find that even you have given out sexual mixed messages at your camp.

Formal Sex Education

The second obstacle to a director's well-considered judgments—lack of knowledge about sex—should come as no surprise when we look at our main sources of information: our parents and the schools.

Parents

Just how much do we learn about sex from our parents? Parents who want to support healthy sexual development are told to engage their children in ongoing age-appropriate dialogue on the topic, but this occurs far less than one would expect.

A look at parent–child dialogues reveals the quantity and quality of sexual knowledge gleaned from parents. Levesque (2000) summarized two major difficulties that come into play:

- Both parents and children find such dialogues uncomfortable, so they occur infrequently. Often the information parents offer is limited to protection from pregnancy and disease, and sometimes the information is either wrong or outdated. A 1998 survey of 1,001 parents by the National Communications Association found that sex was the subject they felt "the least comfortable talking about."

- Parents underestimate the amount of sexual behavior that their children engage in. They believe they know more about their children's sexuality than they really do.

In my own workshops, only rarely does a participant recall having a comprehensive parent-child dialogue about sex. In fact, most participants express surprise over just how little the topic was actually discussed with their parents or their children.

Schools

One might hope that schools would take up the parental slack on teaching human sexuality, but this is wishful thinking. The majority of children in the United States receive either no sex education or an abstinence-only curriculum. Abstinence-only programs focus on refraining from sex as the sole method of avoiding sexual problems. Components of abstinence education, as defined by the United States Congress, include:

- Abstinence from sexual activity outside marriage is the expected standard for all school-age children.

- Sexual activity outside the context of marriage is likely to have harmful psychological and physical effects.

- The exclusive purpose of sex education is to teach the social, psychological, and health gains to be realized by abstinence.

Critics of the abstinence approach claim that its limited perspective and fear tactics in no way prepare children and adolescents for the reality of their sexuality. Research shows that the abstinence approach has not been especially effective in preventing sexual behavior, though a comprehensive approach has been no more effective. As a political battle, though, abstinence education has clearly won. **The vast majority of young people receive no comprehensive sex education.**

We are left with the conclusion that most children reared in the United States receive little formal education on the complexities of human sexuality. Sex is not taught at home or in school. But despite this lack of formal instruction, we all still have knowledge about sex. Where did we get it? Informally, of course.

Informal Sex Education

The four primary sources of "informal" sex education are: friends, the media, our own sexual experiences, and our acceptance of societal norms (Levesque, 2000). Of the four, research shows that peers and the media remain the most accessible sources of information on sex for adolescents. Indeed, both have a greater influence than formal sex education taught in school or by parents.

Peers

Peers are often the main source of information on sex. Adolescents turn to their friends for sexual information far more often that to their parents. Since most of their friends also did not receive a comprehensive sexual education, all have numerous unanswered questions. Peers also affect values and attitudes. As adolescents mature, they rely less on the views of their friends, but especially in younger adolescents the influence of "peer pressure" is quite striking. Children who think their friends are sexually active are more likely to be so themselves.

The problem with relying on friends for sexual information is that they are, at best, limited in the scope of their knowledge and are often wrong. Perhaps you can recall childhood conversations about sex that, in retrospect, were filled with ridiculous assumptions and conclusions. Their collective naivety does not prevent adolescents and even young adults from turning to each other in search of answers.

The Media

Although peers are the most immediate source of direct sexual information, the media may actually have the largest influence on personal views of sexual behavior. Children spend more than forty hours per week watching television, listening to music or the radio, playing video games, and surfing the Internet. This averages out to almost six hours a day of media exposure, and television takes up most of these hours.

Few would argue that sex as depicted on television matches the reality. In a 1989 study of 722 sexual encounters shown on television, only thirteen instances referred to contraception and only eighteen referred to sexually transmitted diseases (Lowry & Towles). A 1993 study found 906 sexual incidents depicted in one week of television programming (Buerkel-Rothfuss). "Responsible" sex was rare. More recent research finds that television rarely refers to sex education, birth control, and abortion. Women are often seen in subservient roles and seeking romance. Music videos are notorious for their sexual content, and films can be even more sexually explicit, many focusing on characters who are overly interested in sex. Research confirms that the media exert an influence on children's values in regard to sexual behavior and gender roles.

Personal Experience

We rely on our own sexual experiences to augment the sexual knowledge base gained from peers and the media. But we should not assume that our own sexual history is like everyone else's. If you started dating early, for example, you may believe that early dating is normal. Your friend who postponed sex until marriage may consider this to be appropriate sexual behavior for everyone. Our upbringing and culture exist in a specific time frame. Even our genes have an influence, as some people are hard-wired to seek high amounts of stimulation, which may show up as a greater number of sexual experiences. We should not blindly accept our own experiences as the norm for our campers, staff, and even our own children.

Social Norms

Finally, our knowledge of sex is supplemented by acceptance of society's norms. We learn early on that certain sexual behaviors are normal and others are not. But "normal" is not a scientific term. Society's definitions of normal and abnormal can change very quickly. Take masturbation, for instance. Well into the last century, people thought masturbation was not only abnormal but downright dangerous. Consider this passage from the major medical work on masturbation, Samuel Tissot's *L'Onanisme* (1760):

> The body loses all of its strength; the growth of those who indulge in these abominable practices before they reach their full height is significantly stunted…. Almost all become hypochondriacs or hysterics, and are afflicted by all the troubles that accompany these unfortunate conditions: sadness, sighs, tears, palpitations, choking, fits, fainting spells…. For others, coughing fits, slow fevers, consumption are the wages of their sin.

Modern readers scoff when they encounter such material, but many still believe that masturbation poses health problems, even though far less drastic. Not too long ago, children caught masturbating or fondling themselves were subjected to punishment. They had their hands tied to their beds and occasionally endured surgical procedures on the penis or clitoris to reduce physical arousal. Today masturbation is no longer considered "abnormal."

Homosexuality is another sexual behavior that is gradually becoming less "abnormal"—too slowly for some, and far too quickly for others. Only a few decades have passed since homosexuality was removed from the official listing of psychological diagnoses. What we are learning from genetic studies suggests that homosexuality may even have a genetic component. Thus society is moving homosexuality toward the "normal" end of the behavior range, supported by both psychological and physiological evidence. All in all, we cannot assume that today's "abnormal" sexual behaviors are necessarily so, since in time society can change its perception.

So far we have observed that most children learn about sex through informal means. The two sources that should be best suited to conduct formal sex education—

parents and schools—are woefully unprepared for that role, so children rely on other sources. But sex information from friends, the media, our own experiences, and societal norms are full of misconceptions, inaccuracies, and even purposefully distorted facts. No wonder so many otherwise intelligent, educated adults have a limited comprehension.

Examining the "Facts"

Can we pinpoint which sexual behavior problems are prevalent in camp settings? We know which problems occur on a regular basis in our own camps, and these might even match those of some of our colleagues. But do our problems reflect what is happening in camps throughout the nation? And how many such problems occur in camps? Do day camps experience more sexual behavior problems than residential camps? Do camps serving young children experience a different set of sexual behavioral problems than those serving teenagers (or adults)?

We may think we already have the answers, but much of what we think we know may not be based on accurate information. We have seen that many of our sexual values and beliefs grow out of information from friends and the media, even though that information may be wrong. The same goes for our perspective on sexual behaviors in camps.

Media Hype

As an example of how wrong we can be, let's examine a common misconception we have all heard of and possibly act on each year. Every year at Halloween, parents are reminded to check their children's candy for signs of tampering such as poisons, razors, or pins. Emergency rooms make x-ray machines available to inspect trick-or-treat bags for any dangers lurking within. But exactly how many children have actually been the victims of Halloween harm?

Sociologist Joel Best (1985) explored just such a question. Since 1958, authorities have received only seventy-six reports of tampered-with Halloween treats, and the majority were found to be fraudulent claims or out-and-out mistakes. Only three deaths of children were attributed to tainted Halloween candy, and all three reports turned out to be false. One child was intentionally poisoned by his father who then made use of a tainted candy story to cover up his deed. In the second case, a boy found and ingested his uncle's stash of heroin; again the immediate family made use of the tainted candy scenario. The third death involved a girl who had a seizure while out trick-or-treating. Though her family attempted to notify various media that the child had a congenital heart problem—the actual cause of her death—headlines claimed yet another victim of tainted candy.

The "date-rape" drug Rohypnol figures in an example related to camps. In the middle to late 1990s, the media published hundreds of reports that Rohypnol was being used in the sexual assault of females. Although the reports offered numerous statistics and quotes, the actual rate of use of this substance for rape was simply unknown. Glassner (1999) took a personal interest in this story and attempted to locate facts to substantiate or negate the hype that the drug was receiving in the press. He could locate only *one* source of information: The Swiss pharmaceutical company that makes the drug asked rape victims who believed they had been given Rohypnol to provide a sample of their urine for analysis. Of the 1,033 samples submitted, only one contained the drug.

During my consulting with camps during the 1990s, I witnessed a steady increase in concern about Rohypnol. Any drugs found on kids—prescription or not—were immediately thought to be "suspicious." We all know campers are supposed to hand in their drugs at the beginning of camp, but we also know that children who think themselves mature enough to manage their own medications are quite capable of "smuggling" a drug through the camp's hectic check-in procedures. For camp officials to jump to the conclusion that such children would use their drugs for the purpose of rape is ridiculous. Yet, with the news frenzy then occurring over Rohypnol, it was almost impossible not to view any drug with suspicion. The use of Rohypnol in sex crimes remained the exception more than the rule and did not deserve the attention it received in camps.

A more current worry for directors, at least if the media coverage is to be believed, is the use of the Internet to abduct children. "Cyber predators," as they are called by some politicians, prey on children who have unsupervised use of the Internet. Major newspaper and television exposés have focused on this threat. A certain number of Internet-based child abductions do occur, but in many instances in which a "predator" makes contact with youth, the "youth" turn out to be undercover agents of the law or reporters. If one subtracts these incidents from the total, the number of cases drops steeply. Many of the supposed adults seeking a sexual relationship on the Internet turn out to be teenagers themselves. No matter how low the actual number of Internet-based abductions, camps with Internet access have had to deal with the vocal concerns of parents. They have installed filters to block adult sites, and some camps have made it a policy to review e-mail to ensure the safety of their campers.

As these examples show, **camps tend to focus on sexual issues that have high media visibility but a low probability of occurrence**. This can have the effect of crowding out attention to the statistically more common sexual behavior problems.

Supposedly one of the most pressing sexual problems in camps today is child molestation. Camps are inundated with materials to help them defend against such predators. But do we actually know how many children have been molested in camps? Is child molestation more common than staff sexual assaults on each other? Is child molestation more common than children sexually assaulting each other in camp settings? How can we say child molestation is the most prevalent sexually inappropriate behavior in camps without the data to prove it?

Inadequate Statistics

Before we can take action to address sexual behavior problems occurring in camps, we must decide which *specific* sexual behavior problems those actions will address. Will it be Rohypnol-based sexual assaults? Sexual predators contacting campers through a camp computer? Staff use of the computer to download pornography? Child molesters grooming their intended victims? We know that sexual activity is bound to occur in camps in some form or other, so what form should we be especially wary of?

Camp professionals would welcome the guidance provided by accurate statistics about sexual behavior occurring in camps. To my knowledge, however, no agency has actually contacted camp directors to ask how many sexually inappropriate behaviors they have encountered in their camps. Lacking systematic studies, we must look to indirect sources of data such as *The CampLine*. This is the American Camping Association's annual account of calls to the ACA hotline for camp-related problems. During the summer of 2002, the hotline received eleven reports of alleged sexual abuse: three staff-to-camper, three staff-to-staff, and five camper-to-camper incidents (Scanlin, 2002). The 2003 edition posted four camper-to-camper and two staff-to-camper incidents (Scanlin, 2003). No doubt these seventeen voluntary reports to the ACA hotline do not represent every incident of sexual misconduct that occurred in the summers of 2002 and 2003. Camps may have purposely refrained from reporting such incidents, or, more likely, such incidents were never brought to the attention of camp administrators.

Another indirect indicator is the number of sex-related incidents reported to camp insurance agencies and to the police. Markel, a major camp insurer, is said to have received twenty-four reports from children who claimed they were sexually abused at camps (Kiger & Sorgen, 2000).

Sooner or later, camps will be called upon to thoroughly investigate the situation. This may come about because directors recognize the need for such data and initiate a voluntary self-study. More likely, a major incident will receive media attention and force an immediate response by the camping industry. The process for this investigation will be nothing short of fascinating. How will sexually inappropriate behavior be defined? How will the study proceed? How will the results be interpreted? Until such investigation takes place, we are left with no means to pinpoint the extent and variety of sexual behaviors in camps.

In the meantime, as we delve into specific sexual behaviors in Chapters 4 through 7, we will relate our meager camp statistics to the results of research on sexual behaviors in society at large. Our task will be to ask how the findings from these studies apply to incidents we might encounter in camps.

Examining Our Personal Beliefs

In staff training for a child advocacy agency, I cited the example of a camp director who discovered that his counselor-in-training, a fifteen-year-old male, had been having a romantic sexual affair with a female camper of the same age. I asked the agency staff to say how they would respond to such a discovery. It was not long before the room split into different factions. Some wanted the male removed from camp. Others wanted both individuals removed from camp. Some thought nothing should be done as long as there was no evidence of coercion in the relationship. Each faction presented compelling evidence for the correctness of their decision, and each was certain that their group had the made the best decision.

Faced with the same dilemma, how could a group of such educated people come to such contrasting solutions? Ross (1994) suggests the reason: "We live in a world of self-generating beliefs which remain largely untested. We adopt those beliefs because they are based on conclusions that are inferred from what we observe, plus our past experience" (p. 242). To paraphrase Ross, we think our beliefs must be the objective truth. By extension, our beliefs about sex and sexuality must also be the objective truth. But as we have seen, our take on the truth is more often a reflection of our own upbringing, experiences, and values than a reflection of reality.

We often respond to the sexual situations we encounter in camps in ways that reflect our personal beliefs rather than our careful thinking. The faulty data that shaped our values, attitudes, and beliefs about sex may lead us to misdiagnose sexual situations and respond in unconstructive ways. A camp director's best defense against this is to look closely at his or her beliefs and values with regard to sex and sexuality.

To assist you in this self-examination, we provide next a series of exercises incorporating surveys and worksheets found in an Appendix at the back of this book. I believe you will be challenged and enlightened by the opportunity they provide for self-examination, and I urge you to complete them. The exercises ask you to examine your values and beliefs about sex and look at your own sexual behaviors. The tools provided help you investigate how you developed such characteristics. After completing the exercises, you will be better prepared to make long-standing positive changes in your camp in regard to sexual activity, but the payoff for this self-examination will be realized in your personal development as well.

The exercises are adapted from workbooks by Toni Cavanagh Johnson, *Treatment Exercises for Child Abuse Victims and Children with Sexual Behavior Problems* (1998) and *Sexuality Curriculum for Abused Children and Young Adolescents and Their Parents* (1999). I have successfully used the exercises in trainings for parents, teenagers, clinicians, camp conferences, and camp staff in-services. Do not approach these as tests that can be failed but as tools of understanding. I caution that some of the questions are graphic and very personal. Do not let this hinder your self-exploration. Take them as a reminder that many people find questions about sex uncomfortable.

	Transmission of Values, Attitudes, and Feelings Regarding Sex and Sexuality
Objectives	To evaluate your values, attitudes, and feelings regarding sex and sexuality. To discover how values, attitudes, and feelings regarding sex and sexuality are developed. To explore sources of influence, other than parents, that affect your development of values, attitudes, and feelings regarding sex and sexuality. To discover how values, attitudes, and feelings regarding sex and sexuality are transmitted to others.
Rationale and Purpose	Some parents do not realize how much their behavior influences their children. They believe that what they say and how they punish misdeeds has more influence. Children's attitudes and values are greatly influenced by their parents' actions. It is important to recognize how our own values and attitudes were shaped by parental influences.
Materials	Exercise: *Mom and Dad Said* (see Appendix)
Instructions	Complete the exercise *Mom and Dad Said*. The issues addressed in this exercise can be used as a springboard for further questions such as: • Which of your ideas about sex are the same as your parents'? Which are different? • For those ideas that are the same as your parents', did you accept them as they were given? Or did you think about them and then accept them? • Did your parents tell you their ideas about sex? Or did you have to guess from their behaviors or things they said? • How did your peers influence your ideas about sex? • How have movies, television, and printed materials shaped your ideas about sex? • Has any religious organization had an influence? • Do your ideas about sex stay the same all the time or change with the situation?

	Values, Attitudes, and Feelings Regarding Sex and Sexuality
Objective	To stimulate your thinking about values, attitudes, and feelings regarding sex and sexuality.
Rationale and Purpose	Clarification of values, attitudes, and feelings about sex and sexuality helps to guide future behavior. The exercise may lead you to modify your behavior and think more carefully about your attitudes.
Materials	Questionnaire: *Values, Attitudes, and Feelings Regarding Sex and Sexuality* (see Appendix)
Instructions	Complete the questionnaire. Use your responses to answer the following questions: • Which questions were hardest to answer? • Which were the easiest? • Which were questions you never thought about before? • Would your own children be surprised by your responses? • Would your co-workers be surprised by your responses? • Do you wonder if other people answer the same way as you? • Do any of your answers go against your religious beliefs? • Do you wish some of your answers were different?

	Analyzing Our Values, Attitudes, and Feelings Regarding Sex and Sexuality
Objective	To encourage you to analyze your values, attitudes, and feelings regarding sex and sexuality.
Rationale and Purpose	Sexual topics are difficult to discuss. The more you are able to discuss your personal sexuality, the more likely you can discuss sex in healthy ways in the numerous environments you inhabit. This exercise helps you explore your own values and attitudes in several topics related to sex and sexuality.
Materials	Worksheet: *Analyzing Our Values, Attitudes, and Feelings Regarding Sex and Sexuality* (see Appendix)
Instructions	Answer the questions.

	Adults' Sexual Behaviors as Children
Objective	To gather information on your sexual behaviors when you were under thirteen years of age. To help you better understand your personal concept of "normal" childhood sexual behavior.
Rationale and Purpose	People have widely differing views about children engaging in sexual behaviors. Each person's own history contributes to his or her perspective on childhood sexuality. A person who did not engage in sexual behaviors when young will likely have a different reaction to childhood sexuality than a person who did engage in such behavior. The questionnaire enables you to gather and recall specifics of your own childhood sexual experiences.
Materials	Questionnaire: *Adults' Sexual Behaviors as Children* (see Appendix)
Instructions	Complete the questionnaire. Compare your responses to those of 352 mental health and child welfare workers (see Appendix).

	Family Roles, Relationships, Behaviors, and Practices
Objective	To make you aware of your own and others' emotional, physical, and sexual boundaries.
	To identify factors that contribute to or cause sexual behaviors in children.
Rationale and Purpose	One task for parents is to teach children about their own rights to "personal space" and physical privacy as well as the rights of others. In some families, people do not have a right to physical privacy. Children are often confused about privacy due to the lack of clarity in their homes.
	Personal space is an area around a person that doesn't have a measurement, but he or she knows when it has been invaded. Some children do not learn about the need for personal space, either other people's or their own.
	Emotional boundaries are violated when a person cannot have private thoughts and when others' feelings are projected onto them.
	It is important to recognize cultural factors when assessing people's family rules, roles, relationships, and boundary practices. Behavior that varies from that of the dominant culture may be considered normal in another culture.
Materials	Questionnaire: *Family Roles, Relationships, Behaviors, and Practices* (see Appendix)
Instructions	The questionnaire has two columns. The left-hand questions ask about the home you were raised in. The right-hand questions ask about your current home. Check the appropriate boxes.
	Be aware that you may not see boundary issues as problematic. Some people raised in boundary-confused environments do not know what a healthy boundary looks like.

*A successful camp is built
on relationships, and relationships can
lead to sexual intimacy.*

2

Three Misconceptions

If you have glanced at Chapter 1 and tried at least some of the exercises, you have made some progress with our first goal: to understand how personal values and beliefs influence people's reactions to sex and sexuality in camps. We will continue to challenge your own beliefs and values throughout this book. For example, many adults are disconcerted to learn what is considered normative (expected) sexual behavior for children. As you read about this in Chapter 6, you may find you need to revisit your own beliefs.

Now we begin work on our second goal: creating a camp environment and culture less conducive to inappropriate sexual behavior. Our first task is to dispel three misconceptions commonly held in the camping industry. Each of these poses a challenge to the adoption of a constructive approach to sexuality in camps.

---

1. We can offer complete safety to camp participants.

2. Sex should not occur in camps.

3. Sex can be prevented in camps.

The Promise of Safety

As I write this chapter, the government has issued a Code Orange terrorist alert. The increased probability of some type of terrorist attack is the top news story on television. Journalists are asking politicians, crisis experts, and sometimes a man or woman in the street just how the average American should respond. The common refrain: Be vigilant. Exercise caution. Don't hesitate to contact the authorities if anything suspicious is observed. But occasionally, one daring person states the obvious truth: There may be little we can do.

Our limited ability to prevent harm is certainly familiar to camp professionals. In my younger days as a camp counselor, I saw directors trying to skirt the issue on parent visiting days. A director would proudly describe all the safety precautions in place, attempting to reassure hesitant parents. Not once did I hear a director directly admit that there was really only so much we could do. Lightning could kill a person. A child could drown in the lake. A teenager could come home from camp with a sexually transmitted disease through an encounter with a peer.

I do not mean to suggest that camp directors deliberately hide the truth about camp safety. Their position is more akin to a state of denial. As I meet more camp professionals through consulting and conference work, I realize that many admit they *cannot* offer complete and utter safety to all camp participants. Unfortunately, many directors continue to suggest that absolute safety is possible.

It is not only camp directors who deny a level of risk. Parents deny it too, as Ditter (2003) points out.

> Some parents do worry too much about their children. On the other hand, reading the news today, many parents feel helpless about protecting their children from the dangers of the world. I would say than an increasing number of parents send their children to camp partly as a way of getting them out of the mainstream culture and into a place where they

are sheltered and well supervised. Indeed, one of the reasons parents react so strongly to any news that suggests their child isn't doing well at camp is because they have their heart set on camp being that refuge and safe place. This is a tall order for directors to fill (p. 52).

Fashioning camps as shelters from the mainstream culture is indeed a "tall order." To say that camps can offer sanctuary to participants is misleading to participants, parents, and the directors themselves. Camps can and do offer new experiences and the potential for developmental growth, but they cannot and should not be marketed as refuges from the dangers of the world.

Even with the most stringent of safety precautions, each year children will be hurt—and even killed—in camps. A great many more will have a less-than-wonderful experience and wish never to attend camp again. Some will be homesick, developmentally immature for the camp experience, or just not a good fit with the chosen camp. Others will be bullied and mistreated both physically and psychologically by peers and staff. Staff, too, may experience distress and mistreatment. Some of these individuals—both staff and campers—will have a sexual encounter with harmful consequences.

We cannot promise parents that their children will not be harmed at camp. We can promise only that we will do our best to prevent such harm. Parents who buy into the image of camps as idyllic islands of safety, which some camps actively promote, are at risk for hurt and anger if a problem occurs. Camps are likewise at risk as it becomes evident that they really cannot guarantee the complete safety that many parents desire.

All camp participants—campers, staff, parents, and directors—must to some degree accept the unknowable for camps to proceed. This lack of certainty from year to year is one of the most stressful yet exciting experiences for each camp director. I once heard a staff member say he sometimes wished that the children would always behave and that fellow staff members were always consistent. After a few seconds, though, he reminded himself that, if his wish came true, camp would likely be boring. Given a choice, most camp staff would rather endure an element of risk than face a season of unmitigated boredom.

The Inevitability of Relationships

Sex will occur in camps. There is really nothing else to say about it. But I often encounter camp professionals who say sex must be stopped because it poses a grave danger to the camp's reputation or to its day-to-day functioning. In this section you will see that, despite a camp director's most earnest belief that sex should not occur in camps, it inevitably will.

Many camp directors are of two minds about camp relationships. They certainly desire teamwork and camaraderie among staff. Even more, they understand the value of appropriate relationships between campers and staff, for such relationships are a foundation of the camp experience and a mainstay of the camping industry. Still, many camp directors express concern and frustration with relationships of all types in camps, and any seasoned camp director can appreciate their dilemma.

Directors are all too familiar with the romantic squabbles of camp counselor couples, but there are plenty of problems with non-romantic staff relationships too: This counselor cannot tolerate her unit leader. This specialist does not like the assistant director. This counselor refuses to co-host the talent show with another staffer at whom he is angry.

Difficulties in camper relationships are also common: A unit of boys bonds so well with each other that they now belittle any camper not fortunate enough to be among their ranks. Two campers have to be placed in separate cabins because of their constant fighting. Parents request that campers who were friends back home must not only be placed in the same unit, but must be assigned adjoining beds in the same cabin.

Finally, relationships between staff and campers can pose problems. A strong connection between staff and campers is a priority for all camps, but at least once a season some camper comes to believe that a staff member is purposefully making his life miserable, or a counselor threatens to quit if a certain camper is not removed from his cabin.

Camp environments embody relationships of many types. Such relationships can assist in the smooth running of the camp, or they can be a source of endless stress for the administration. No wonder many directors wish for staff members who can build bonds instantly with campers but keep those relations professional and respectfully distant. If staff could just develop cooperative working relationships amongst themselves and with campers, many of the problems inherent in camp life would vanish. Unfortunately, such an ideal is rarely encountered in real life. A director who expects camp to run like a well-oiled machine will be sorely disappointed as relationships and their complications disrupt his or her best intentions. **A successful camp is built on relationships of many sorts among many participants. Relationships must be nurtured no matter how stressful they may be on occasion.**

Role in Happiness and Job Satisfaction

There's a good reason why I place such strong emphasis on relationships for camp success. Let's take a brief side trip into the study of human happiness. Historically, psychologists have focused on disorders of the human psyche and methods to "heal" them. Putting the spotlight on pathology has left the thriving and positive qualities of the human mind in the shadows. Psychologists have now realized the limits of their focus on the negatives of human behavior, and determined researchers have made it their mission to explore the positive aspects of human behavior that make life worth living.

Some of the findings of this positive approach to psychology surprise nobody, while other findings come as quite a revelation. Take money for instance. Surveys conducted over the past twenty years show that most of the Western world is convinced that money can buy happiness. Researchers examining the link between money and happiness have drawn some sobering conclusions. The most relevant is that increased wealth brings no increase in feelings of well-being:

> [I]nhabitants of the wealthiest industrialized Western nations are living in a period of unprecedented riches, in conditions that previous generations would have considered luxuriously comfortable, in relative peace and security, and they are living on the average close to twice as long as their grandparents did. Yet, despite all these improvements in material conditions, it does not seem that people are so much more satisfied with their lives than they were before (Csikszentmihalyi, 1999, p. 822).

The research indicates that, although we may be twice as wealthy, we are not twice as happy. Nor do factors such as age, education level, gender, physical attractiveness, and intelligence have much effect on happiness. Even race has little effect, though it has slightly more than the other factors.

So which external factors *do* affect happiness and satisfaction in life? Two of them are the topic of this book—relationships and work. Several characteristics of the work place affect life satisfaction (Griffeth & Hom, 2001):

- Autonomy; the opportunity for personal control.

- Variety in job content and skill use.

- Supportive supervision.

- Opportunity for interpersonal contact; a comfortable combination of privacy and social contact with others.

This list is not exhaustive, but I draw your attention to the characteristic "opportunity for interpersonal contact." Affiliation with others is not just a superficial aspect of work life; it is a significant variable in job satisfaction. In fact, relationships are essential in all spheres of our existence—work, family, and leisure. **Close relationships and faith relationships appear to be the greatest external influences on personal satisfaction with life.**

Family and Social Ties

Most of you reading this book already understand the importance of relationships in our lives. Those of you who took a basic psychology class in college can probably recall Harry Harlow's experiments. When forced to choose between cuddling and eating, infant monkeys preferred to cuddle with a surrogate mother—basically, a rolled up towel with a clown face. Or you may recall pediatrician Henry Chapin's report regarding the children's hospitals and orphanages of 1915. Children under two, taken care of in all respects except for adequate physical touch, were found to be wasting away.

Unlike most other living creatures, humans are born with a relatively immature brain. There is a good reason for this. If the brain were to develop its full complexity and size while still within the womb, the infant's head would not be able to pass through the birth canal at delivery. Only recently have the implications of this become apparent.

Since most of the brain matures outside the womb, early experiences have a dramatic influence on the future of the individual:

> Love, and the lack of it, change the young brain forever. The nervous system was once thought to unfold into maturity in accordance with the instructions in its DNA, much as a person alone in a room might, with a set of directions and a flurry of creases, produce an origami swan. But as we know now, most of the nervous system needs exposure to crucial experience to drive its healthy growth (Lewis, Amini, & Lannon, 2000, p. 89).

A close relationship with a parent or parents has a direct effect on the infant's brain development. Just think of it. A healthy parent-infant relationship actually affects the physiological growth of the brain!

The effect of relationships on brain functioning does not end with childhood. It is becoming clear that we need relationships to maintain our ongoing physical and mental health. Recent studies of people with leukemia, heart disease, and immune system disorders have shown that patients with little social support have the worst outcomes. Relationships may have an even greater effect on psychological health. The entire therapy industry is based on the premise that beneficial change best occurs within a relationship with a supportive and understanding therapist.

Consider what the death of a loved one—the loss of treasured relationship—does to our mental and physical functioning:

> Anyone who has grieved a death has known despair from the inside: the leaden inertia of the body, the global indifference to anything but the loss, the aversion to food, the urge to closet oneself away, the inability to sleep, the relentless grayness of the world (Lewis, Amini, & Lannon, 2000, p. 79).

Societies throughout history and all over the world have formed relationships. Scientists reason that our ancestors formed relationships for increased safety and survival. Many creatures spend their lives surrounded by others of their species, recalling the old adage, "safety in numbers." Relationships made early humans more successful in hunting and agriculture, and enabled them to overpower enemies who competed for the same food and shelter. Individuals preferring a solitary existence fared far worse than those who lived in groups. Thus the disposition for group living was more successfully passed down through the generations than the disposition for social isolation.

Camp directors can see this in-born characteristic operating during the first few days of camp. New staff members seek out alliances with others to reduce the uncertainty of the new environment. Returning staff almost instantly re-create alliances from the previous season as they evaluate the new staff members. Even directors are not immune to the slight anxiety of the new season and seek subtle reassurance in those they know and trust. For the first two weeks or so, they tend to spend a little more time with returning staff than with new staff, and they request the opinions and feedback of returning staff much more.

We have seen that relationships influence life satisfaction and have positive effects on health. We have also seen that the need for relationships is molded into our very genetic structure.

> We humans feel motivated to eat, to drink, to have sex, and to achieve. But being what Aristotle called "the social animal," we also have a need to belong, to feel connected with others in enduring, close relationships (Myers, 1999, p. 374).

As an interesting parallel, consider a review by Buck (2002) of biologists' recent findings suggesting that genes survive only in the company of other genes. The very building blocks of our physiology thrive on inter-cooperation to accomplish their tasks.

Just as feeling connected to others has invaluable effects on humans, a lack of connectedness can have harmful effects.

> Out of the need to define a "we" comes loving families, faithful friendships, fraternal organizations, and team spirit, but also teen gangs, isolationist cults, ethnic hostilities, and fanatical nationalism. Because the fear of aloneness sometimes seems worse than the pain of emotional or physical abuse, attachments may also keep people in degrading relationships. When our social ties are threatened or broken, negative emotions may overwhelm us. Exile, imprisonment, and solitary confinement are progressively more severe forms of punishment. Recently bereaved individuals often find life empty and pointless. Those denied others' acceptance and inclusion may feel depressed. Anxiety, jealousy, loneliness, and guilt all involve disruptions to the human need to belong (Myers, 2000, p. 62).

With our in-born drive to connect to others, it should not surprise us that camp participants become involved in myriad non-romantic and non-sexual relationships. It is only human to do so. And once these relationships have formed, some of them will invariably progress to become sexual in nature.

The Progression of Intimacy

There exists a recognized progression from a first meeting with another person to a sexual experience, though most of us could not clearly describe it. Camp directors know this from recalling their own romantic experiences. Our camp participants do not form sexual liaisons on the very night of their arrival. They engage in a pattern of increasingly sexualized verbal and physical behaviors. The typical steps are shown here:

finding another person attractive → going on dates → holding hands →

kissing → touching/fondling → sexual intercourse

This progression can last anywhere from days to years. Research shows that some demographic groups move through the steps more quickly than others, yet most follow the same sequence.

An important characteristic of this progression is the increasing intimacy of the relationship. Unless two individuals get to know one another, there is little chance of forward movement. Thus couples spend much of the early dating stages sharing their dreams, aspirations, personal histories, and any and all information that each believes is relevant. I can recall from my early camp counselor days the many couples who would sit by the waterfront night after night discussing an apparently endless number of personal topics. As a camp director, almost two decades later, I still witness strikingly similar behavior among the camp staff.

As couples become increasingly intimate through verbal means, their intimacy enters the physical realm. Holding hands and casual kissing open the door to more sexualized activities that enable the couple to experience more intimacy. As intimacy increases, so does trust, and this paves the way for even more intimate behaviors. Some of the couples I see on the waterfront today are bound to become sexual partners by the end of the season, following the same progression as when I was a young camp counselor. Our lives as camp directors would certainly be easier if camp participants never progressed past the step of finding another person attractive. Fortunately, many do stop there, but many others do not.

We have seen that relationships are bound to occur in camps, and as they increase in intimacy some relationships will progress to sexual behavior. Directors who steadfastly hold to the belief that sex should not occur in camps are engaging in wishful thinking. In fact, our understanding of human sexuality suggests the opposite, that there is every reason to believe that sex will be present in one form or another in all camps.

Stamping Out Sex

Camp directors can certainly try to stamp out all forms of human sexuality in camps, but there is really no way this can be accomplished. No intervention will dramatically decrease the amount of sexual contact between individuals. Still, directors persist in formulating policies outlawing sexual behavior, the formation of intimate relationships, and even the most casual displays of romantic affection such as holding hands.

I was saddened to learn that the "first night sex talk" is still used in some camps. I myself was an unwilling participant in many such talks in my early camping years. Males and females would be separated on the first night of staff orientation. The camp director, often in tandem with the camp nurse, would visit each group and explain the hazards of sex and romance in camps. Some directors would use tactful language in discussing the topic; others would use language that shocked me. How successful is such an intervention? The common response by staff was to listen respectfully to the camp director and, when the talk was over, proceed to the center of the campgrounds to meet up with the opposite sex!

To my amusement, after I took over the directorship of a camp, a long-time staff member asked if the first night sex talk would continue. Though freely admitting that the talk accomplished nothing, she thought it at least set the tone that the camp administration frowned upon sex.

A camp director can certainly set a tone for acceptance or non-acceptance of human sexuality. Staff in particular will quickly recognize the camp director's beliefs about sexuality and either become more comfortable in expressing their sexuality or take it deeper into hiding. What will not cease, though, is human sexuality. Any attempt to block it is destined to fail.

There are four primary reasons why a director cannot eradicate sex in camps. Each reason is a powerful counterbalance to any attempt at repression by a camp administration.

1. Our genes dictate a need for relationships, intimacy, and sex.

2. Camps foster intimacy.

3. Camps are romantic environments.

4. Sex is practically impossible to monitor.

The Genetic Plan

Attempts to stop relationships and sex are, in reality, battles against our very own genetic history. Just as the need for relationships is built into our genes, so too is a sexual appetite. Humans are programmed to be sexual beings. It is built into our very instincts to be sexually aroused and seek corresponding outlets. Granted, some people enter camp with better control of their sexual impulses but, even then, sexuality has not disappeared.

Sexuality assumes no less a role than do relationships in the history of humanity. We already know that humans have specific drives hardwired in the brain. The need for food is an obvious example—without food, we would die. The need and desire for sex is likewise hardwired into the human brain. If our ancestors had opted for the celibate life, we would not exist. Sex allows the continuation of the species.

Every person is a sexual being. You already know this about yourself, but it applies to your staff and campers as well. And not only those who have gone through puberty are sexual beings. Even infants and young children have sexual aspects to their behavior. From our earliest moments of life we are in many ways sexual beings, and this continues throughout our lifespan. All participants entering the camp environment—from the youngest campers to the most mature staff members—experience sexual stimulation and pleasure arising from their bodies. Depending on their physical and cognitive maturity, they may also experience sexual urges and desires of varying intensity.

Your staff, your campers, and even you were fashioned by a genetic plan that places much emphasis on sex. While staff and older campers may experience different sexual urges than the youngest members, some form of sexuality occurs at every age level. Young campers seem to be on a perpetual quest for information about sex and body parts. Due to the number of nerve connections in the body geared for sex, they also know the pleasure that touching themselves can bring. It is only to be expected that sex and sexuality will enter the camp environment—there is no way they cannot. As Blackmore (1999) has stated, our "genetic evolution has created brains that are especially concerned with sex, food, and power" (p.121).[*] All three of these drives played an indispensable role in our survival as a species.

An Essential Intimacy

The second reason camp directors cannot stamp out sex is that intimacy is integral to the camp experience. How successful is a camp where staff make no attempt to get to know one another? What parents would send their children to a camp where staff do not have meaningful contact with the campers? An expectation for camp staff is that they will involve themselves in significant relationships with campers. Especially at the unit level, staff are expected to bond with campers to form a cohesive team. We want staff to get to know one another and the campers that they serve, but there are consequences: **The very intimacy that we seek to build is the seedling for future sexual relationships.** Recall that we defined intimacy as the sharing of information of an increasingly personal nature.

---

[*]From Susan Blackmore, *The Meme Machine.* Copyright ©1999. Reprinted by permission of Oxford University Press.

The fact is camps are hyper-intimate environments. Comparing camp employ-ment with non-camp employment, I see a striking difference in the first day of work. In a non-camp job, I am usually given an office and a chance to move in, and my co-workers stop by to introduce themselves as the day progresses. Contrast this to a typical camp job. Within the first hour, there are icebreakers and team-building exercises. Every attempt is made to foster positive interpersonal relationships. Once people become more comfortable with each other, the stage is set for romantic relationships to form.

One camp director gave me a wonderful example of the unintended effects of the hyper-intimacy of camp life. The first two days of his staff orientation had been hindered by severe thunderstorms. By the third evening, the weather had cleared enough for the traditional staff camping trip. At the onset of the trip, the staff had barely bonded, and there was much silence on the two-mile hike to the designated site. How-ever, that night, with clear weather and a beautiful view of the starry sky overhead, the staff began to talk amongst themselves. Most of the staff even declined to go to sleep that night. They sat around the fire and discussed their histories and their aspirations.

The camp director and his two program directors were overjoyed—the staff was finally bonding. The next day revealed the benefits of this intimacy. There was laughter, rapport, and an obvious interest in the camp's mission. But there was also an unexpected effect: The very next evening, six staff members were found to be out past curfew. Three couples had formed during the overnighter. In the midst of their early infatuation, each couple found it necessary to be with each other in spite of the camp's curfew policy.

In none of my other professional jobs have I seen my co-workers in a bathing suit. Nor have I seen them perform in a talent show or sing a grace at mealtime before hundreds of people. I could not tell you what my professional co-workers look like by firelight or by the light of the moon.

By their nature, camps offer physical environments and programming that are highly conducive to intimacy, and camp staff get to know one another very quickly as a result. The routine of daily camp life presents opportunities and challenges that galvanize camaraderie. It also presents stressors that support such cohesion. Residential camps in which staff do not return home for a period of time further incubate increased intimacy.

We can assume that what camp directors are hoping for is *selective* intimacy. If staff could use their obvious interpersonal skills just enough to bond with children and just enough to create a functioning team spirit, the problems of camp romance would not have to surface. Unfortunately, this is not realistic. Once we initiate those icebreakers and team-building exercises, we are in the process of supporting future romantic relationships. As people begin to work together and share increasing amounts of personal information, chances for romantic intimacy appear. Intimacy is built into the entire camp experience. Once staff members get to know one another—a stated camp goal—couples will form and many will progress to sexual behavior.

A Setting for Romance

Another obstacle exists to regulating sexuality out of camps: **Camps are the ultimate romantic environment.** One camp in which I worked was a few short miles from two honeymoon resorts. The same amenities offered there for a romantic atmosphere were present in the camp: a private lake, acres of lush woodlands, and secluded niches away from the rest of humanity. Camps that work out of college dormitories or church basements may not have these problems, but those of us working in the out-of-doors must admit that our camps have characteristics that foster romance. Sitting on a dock under a full moon with a person to whom one is attracted is certainly a stimulus for increased intimacy.

The dilemma for camp directors is this: They may take proactive steps to limit romantic intimacy, but these steps are stymied by the need for staff to develop sufficient intimacy for teamwork in an environment that is romantically stimulating. When staff arrive for camp, they will necessarily seek out relationships of all types with other people, including members of the opposite sex. Some of these will develop into romantic and sexual relationships. This is inescapable. Even in camps that hire only males or only females, sexual relationships can develop. Attempts to prevent intimate relationships are not only perceived as highly intrusive—and anger provoking—by staff but also go against our own genetic programming.

The Difficulty of Policing Sex

A purely practical problem arises with policies that attempt to negate human sexuality. Just how can we verify that a no-sex policy is successful? How does a director know if a policy has eliminated or even reduced the amount of sexual behavior in camp? Several factors work against being able to police the amount of sex in camp.

- ## Sexual behavior is almost always hidden.

Many staff orientations forbid sexual behavior on camp property, and many directors make clear their negative view of sexual activity. Staff are well aware that they must keep their encounters secret. Most children and teens entering camp have already had it drummed into them that sexual behavior at their age is wrong. They realize that when it occurs it must stay hidden from adults. Finally, people who enter camp with sexual behavior problems, such as sexually aggressive individuals or molesters, know that their behavior is wrong and purposefully camouflage their activities.

With participants camouflaging and concealing their activities, how does a director go about keeping track of the sexual behavior in camp? Whenever a director claims to have created a system that reduces sexual activity in camps, I suspect that the amount of sexual activity has not decreased but has simply been driven underground and out of view of the camp administration.

- ## The camp director can be in only one place at a time.

On a typical camp afternoon, countless events are underway. Some campers are doing arts and crafts, others are swimming. Some staff are preparing the evening meal in the kitchen, while others are taking a needed siesta. Because the camp director has a limited field of vision, he or she has only a inkling of what is happening in camp at any given moment. Somewhere out of the director's sight, sexual activity may be occurring.

- ## Personal expectations control the focus of attention.

Hundreds if not thousands of stimuli clamor for the director's attention. Our physical makeup allows us to focus only on those stimuli in the immediate range of experience. A director sitting in an office may focus on the paperwork, the comfort of the chair, or the sounds of birds outside. Behind the scenes, the director's brain is instantly and automatically screening out the vast majority of stimuli. To focus on all stimuli in the immediate environment would overwhelm the brain. Most humans do not truly appreciate just how adept they are at screening out information. We are usually aware of only a small handful of the stimuli that actively surround us.

Another influence of our brain is that our expectations have dramatic effects on our behavior. People told they were drinking alcohol acted as if they were drunk when, in reality, the liquid contained no alcohol. Subjects developed a skin reaction to a harmless leaf after being informed it was poison ivy.

In combination, our selective attention and our expectations have a strong influence on our perception—we see what we expect to see. For example, camp director Charles expects that his camp will run smoothly this season; yes, there will be some challenges but nothing he can't deal with. Brian, his assistant, expects that people just look out for themselves and require constant supervision to ensure quality work. Their differing expectations affect both their behavior and their perceptions. Charles barely leaves the front office during the season, while Brian goes out to watch the staff in action every day. At the end of the season, director Charles congratulates himself on hiring such an excellent staff, whereas Brian says he would never hire back any of these "lazy and self-centered" people.

Because Charles never left the office, he never saw his staff in action. Brian's opinion may be more accurate, but his view, too, is biased. Though Brian monitored the staff daily, we can guess that he did not focus on their numerous positive behaviors. His negative expectation could have blocked him from perceiving the good and even great things the staff did.

With personal expectations holding such power over perception, is it any surprise that a camp director who expects the camp to be safe from sexually inappropriate activity ceases to find any such activity occurring? A camp director who believes that a sexual prevention policy is working is unlikely to seek out the information that could refute this belief.

What to Do?

I hope that the evidence presented here has convinced you that sexual activity cannot be eradicated from camps. Many directors have accepted this, though not necessarily with a sense of satisfaction. Others still believe that, with enough supervision and publicized consequences, camp participants will refrain from sex. We have tried to show that a policy that forbids and criminalizes human sexuality is doomed to failure. Between camp participants' purposeful hiding of sexual behavior and camp leaders' limited field of vision, such a policy has little chance of achieving its aims.

At conferences, I am often pressed to give at least one intervention that will clearly cut down on camp sexual activity. I can give only one piece of advice in good conscience: **Stop trying to eradicate sex in camps!** A far better intervention is to create a camp environment that reduces the risk of inappropriate and damaging sexual behavior. Please note the difference. We openly acknowledge that sexual behavior will occur in camps, that a policy of eliminating sex will be ineffectual, and that not all sexual activity is worthy of concern. Instead, we concentrate our efforts on a far smaller domain, that of inappropriate sexual behaviors and those that can cause the most problems for a camp.

The next chapter looks at general factors that increase safety in camps. A camp that does not offer a safe environment for participants places them at risk of sexual harm. The final chapter of this book presents concrete steps to reduce the specific risk of sexual harm.

For those of you who still think you can outlaw sexual behavior in camp, I leave you with one final observation. Researchers have shed light on the major influences that determine when young people begin to engage in sexual activity (Levesque, 2000). On a hierarchy of influences, the top three are friends, a person's romantic partner, and the media. Where do parents stand on this hierarchy? The fact is, parents rank quite low, even parents who are quite adamant in their disapproval of sex. No camp directors that I know would ever suggest they have a stronger influence than parents. So what makes us think we could ever successfully enforce a no-sex policy?

The camp environment exerts a powerful influence on the amount of inappropriate sexual behavior.

3
A Culture of Safety and Respect

Although sexual activity will never be eradicated completely from camps, there are steps directors can take to minimize the amount of *inappropriate* sexual behavior. The first step is to make sure the camp promotes a culture of safety and respect. This chapter lays a foundation for overall physical and psychological safety in camps. Without such a foundation, there is no use in formulating interventions to minimize inappropriate sexual behaviors. The lack of this underpinning of safety will erode any sex-specific interventions.

Every person who holds a job, whether camp related or not, soon recognizes that the work place lives by two standards—the official policy, or how things are *supposed* to work, and the employees' tacit understanding of how things *really* work. Quite often the unspoken understanding has more influence than the official policy on employee behavior. For example, a written rule may call for employees to be in their work areas by a certain time. Yet if a new employee witnesses her co-workers consistently coming in late with no penalty, she quickly learns that the rule has no legitimacy. After a few weeks she may even start coming in late herself.

I have encountered camps in which rules were officially proclaimed in a staff manual and during staff training but only to appease a board of directors or to meet a requirement of the American Camping Association. The administration never made an effort to enforce the rules.

Some camp administrators present staff with conflicting information about sex. They issue dire warnings against sexual relations in camps, yet they proceed to engage in just such behaviors themselves. Their personal behavior gives staff a green light to ignore the policy manual and follow their example. After all, if the camp director and administrative staff can participate in sexual relationships, why should the rest of the staff have to refrain from sex?

This chapter focuses on how the camp culture—the unspoken rules by which the camp is run—can increase or decrease unwanted behaviors of all kinds, including inappropriate sexual behaviors. Understanding the impact of these unspoken rules is basic to establishing a camp culture of safety and respect.

The Influence of Camp Culture

The camp environment is not simply a passive background for events that occur during a camp season. It has a powerful and continuous influence on camp life. Consider the plight of a camp director who had to endure a new housing development adjoining the boundaries of her camp. The once-private enclave surrounded by acres of wooded area was soon surrounded by family homes. Suddenly the director was besieged with complaints about noise from the camp during the height of the season. "Intruders" from the development constantly entered the camp grounds. The night sky was no longer visible thanks to the bright lights of the planned community. The sounds of radio and television filled the night where once there had been silence and an occasional animal cry.

In this example, the housing development clearly brought unpleasant changes to the physical camp environment, but "environment" can be broadened to include the whole atmosphere of the camp. Such an encompassing perspective looks at the rules and regulations of the camp, its history, customs, rituals, values, and norms. A two-week camp for children with disabilities will have vastly different customs, rituals, values, and norms than a for-profit camp that offers services throughout the year.

When we look at the overall experience of camp for staff and campers, we are actually examining its *culture*. The concept of culture is borrowed from the field of anthropology. Anthropologists study what life is like in other civilizations. Business researchers compare the corporate cultures of specific companies. Each camp, too, has its own unique culture. Following are some aspects of camp culture that can exert a negative influence and make a camp more prone to inappropriate behavior.

Tolerance for Antisocial Activity

A culture that ignores antisocial behavior in general lends itself to the development of sexual behavior problems. Tolerance of mundane violations is the number one camp characteristic that invites antisocial behavior.

Many camps clearly inform staff that romantic relationships are forbidden and could be grounds for termination. Yet, several weeks into camp, after staff have had time to form some intimacy, signs of romantic relationships are downplayed or outright ignored. Allowing staff to hold hands, sit together at camp-wide activities, and display other signs of intimacy gives unspoken approval to the relationship.

A camp that allows mild forms of harassment, such as whistling and leering at other staff while in bathing suits, will be challenged to tackle the more flagrant acts of harassment. Camps that tolerate subtle bullying—staff on staff, camper on camper, and/or staff on camper—are likely to experience more problematic sexual behaviors.

The atmosphere of tolerance for antisocial acts makes it far more difficult for a camper or staff member to report abuse.

Until recently, the U.S. court system tended to treat male juvenile sex offenders in a fairly lenient manner. The thinking behind this was that "boys will be boys" and that sexual aggression against females was a norm for teenage males. Camp directors have expressed the same leniency in response to sexual abuse of female staff, with comments such as "it just got out of hand" and "he didn't mean any harm." Camp directors have even gone to great lengths to protect certain staff members from the repercussions of their actions.

Look past the formal policies in place for problem behaviors at your own camp, and ask yourself whether these policies are actively enforced. The American Camping Association requires a harassment policy in their standards for camps, and many camps have gone to great expense to have lawyers formulate or review their policies. On paper such polices look very official, but are they followed? Are subtle forms of harassment and bullying acted upon? Or are they ignored in the hope that they will disappear, or in the belief that they are not serious acts?

Consequences

Whether your camp follows through on consequences says much about whether the camp culture lends itself to inappropriate sexual behavior.

One camp director told staff during orientation that, if there were any reports of inappropriate sexual behavior, the local state police would be called in to investigate. Midway through the season, a female lifeguard reported that a member of the administrative staff had sexually assaulted her. The female had been "visiting" his bunk in the boys' section of the camp—a definite violation of camp policy. The camp director responded by terminating both employees and having them immediately removed from the camp premises. The woman was told that, if she wanted to press legal charges against the man involved, she would have to do so on her own.

The termination of both employees for violating camp policy was understandable, if not necessarily the best decision. But what about the state police involvement that was promised during staff orientation? Seasoned camp staff can appreciate the action that this camp director took. After all, involving the state police might have created negative publicity for the camp, and no camp director wishes to submit to such an ordeal. On the other hand, why spell out consequences to staff if those consequences are not real?

In another example, a camp director was vocal in his disapproval of camp relationships—such involvements would result in termination. Yet, on a visit to his camp, I saw activities that seemed completely contrary to his warnings. The camp was having a carnival, and each unit had set up a booth such as one might find on a fairground. One unit had established a "love boat" ride in which couples were allowed to row to the middle of the lake together. Another unit had set up a "secret message" booth where a person could write an anonymous private message to another person and have it hand-delivered by a camper or staff member working the booth. The number of sexually graphic messages sent amongst staff members was alarming! The camp director did not close these booths, nor did he approach the staff to question their motivation for establishing these activities.

Directors should especially heed the advice they give staff in regard to discipline with children: Do not threaten consequences that will not truly occur. If staff see that there are no consequences, or that the consequences are not that severe, they are less inclined to avoid inappropriate behaviors. Though I argue against policies that deny camp staff the right to form intimate relationships, camps that do take such an approach must follow through with consequences if the policy is violated.

Enforcing consequences is especially difficult late in the season for many camps. By this point, camps have already lost staff members through terminations and resignations and can ill afford to lose another. Staff are aware of their heightened importance during these last few weeks and sometimes take advantage. Countless directors have told me that, in camps that house both male and female staff members, the last few weeks are rife with sexual relationships. Staff visit each others' cabins after hours and are far more demonstrative of their romantic involvement during the daylight hours. There is no easy solution to this, but simply to ignore policy and consequences certainly damages the camp culture.

Organizational Scrutiny

The effect of organizational scrutiny on the acceptance or rejection of inappropriate behavior should not be downplayed. A camp director who professes not to tolerate any form of sexual harassment but who never mentions the subject again after staff week is not actively preventing harassment. Likewise, camps that forbid staff to be in a cabin with children while they are undressing, but that never monitor whether their policy is being followed, are equally at fault. The more monitoring in camp, the more likely that possible perpetrators will refrain from inappropriate activity. Of course camps are not prisons, and staff may become frustrated at the intrusiveness of camp administration. Directors must find the proper balance between disengagement and overzealousness.

Directors may try to monitor behavior by walking around the camp, but they can take other proactive steps to determine whether inappropriate activity is taking place. Some camps have the staff nurse visit each unit and meet with campers privately to discuss any possible mistreatment. Other camps reverse the age-old policy of minimizing contact between parents and children while the camp season is in session, hoping in this way to expose any incidents of sexually inappropriate behavior. Camp directors cannot simply wait for a victim to seek help voluntarily. Too many camp directors depend solely upon stating an open-door policy during staff week. They think this will cause people who are victimized to come forward. A review of the research literature, though, clearly shows that most victims—especially victims of sexual mistreatment—do not come forward.

Perpetrators who think their offense will be recognized or who are concerned about the consequences are less likely to offend. They will be deterred by an environment where they know the director is watching what goes on. They would be far more comfortable in an environment where the director is overwhelmed and has little time to monitor behavior.

Group Norms

A major factor contributing to inappropriate sexual behavior is group norms. As an example, I have personally witnessed the destructive power of a small faction of staff members. One staff member had such a great experience in camp that he not only returned the following year but also referred a great number of his fraternity brothers. This contingent came into camp with a set of norms that were in opposition to the camp norms. Alcohol use was rampant, though all these men supported each other in denying the activity. Harassment of female staff members and bullying of children was also apparent. When the director finally terminated two of the worst offenders, the entire group quit at the same time. I know this is not an isolated incident, as other camp directors have reported similar problems with tight cliques in the camp environment.

We can generalize the concept of norms to the wider camp environment as well. Some camps thrive under a veil of secrecy. Because negative events reflect badly on the administration, the director tries to control information so that only the most positive aspects of camp life are revealed. The norm in such camps is for staff to work out problems on their own and to disturb the director as little as possible. Such a norm jeopardizes the safety and welfare of all camp participants. Other camps have a norm of minimal supervision. There it is no surprise to find staff members having sex in cabins with children present, cases of camper-on-camper assault, and reported sexual threats on female members. Lastly, some directors should simply not be in the field due to their questionable ethics. These directors pollute the atmosphere of an entire camp and allow norms to be established that work against a satisfying camp experience. Fortunately, the vast majority of camp directors do not resemble these individuals.

Job Stress

An indirect influence on camp culture is job stress. Stress stemming from employment has become a major subject of research and has been found to have innumerable negative effects on physical health, family functioning, and psychological well-being. Anyone who has not worked in a camp environment likely underestimates the amount of stress that comes with a camp position. In interviews for staff positions, one of my favorite questions is to ask the candidate to verbalize his or her understanding of the typical camp day. People who have never worked at camp invariably describe a scenario of unending fun. They vastly underestimate the amount of effort demanded by camp employment.

All camp employment is challenging, stressful, and has many negative aspects to it, but some camps are more stressful than others. Granted, a camp's mission and the specific population it serves can raise the stress level for staff. But the more important determinant of stress and its effect on behavior is supervision. Indeed, the relationship an employee has with his or her supervisor is often the most important factor in day-to-day job satisfaction.

A camp staff member working in a stressful environment with minimal supervisory support, or worse, abusive supervision, will have little opportunity to deal with the stress in productive ways. This is particularly true for residential camps. Everybody can relate to the experience of taking our work-based anger out on family and friends. After a stressful day, we find ourselves less tolerant of our children, spouses, or anybody we spend time with after hours. In the same manner, campers and other staff can become the unintended victims of a staff member's stress and anger at his or her supervisor.

Assessing Your Camp Culture

As we have seen, the culture of a camp plays no small role in setting the stage for sexually inappropriate behavior. Each camp has characteristics that favor such acts, just as each has characteristics that reduce such acts. Camps that pursue a positive camp culture—do not tolerate any form of bullying and harassment, follow their own policies, enforce consequences against antisocial behavior, put security measures in place, act ethically, employ administrative staff that model appropriate behavior, and foster nonabusive management/supervisory practices—such camps create an atmosphere in which inappropriate activities are less likely to flourish.

Where does your own camp stand on these aspects of camp culture? Ask yourself these six questions.

1. Does your camp allow bullying, even subtle or apparently playful types?

2. Does your camp allow harassment, even subtle or apparently playful types?

3. How flexible are your rules, regulations, and policies?

4. How does your camp verify that safety regulations are implemented consistently?

5. How does your camp verify that participants are treated with respect?

6. How does your camp verify that participants feel safe?

How accurately do you think you answered these questions? If you asked the same six questions of all camp participants—administration, campers, and staff—would they answer the same as you? To get a true picture of your camp culture, your own impressions may not be enough. Let us explore some of the reasons.

A Director's View

We expect the top person in any organization—CEO, president, or camp director—to be the person with the most knowledge about what goes on in the organization. But this may not be true. Having worked as a camp counselor and specialist, I can easily recall information that was never known by the director and administrative staff yet was known by most of the other staff. We knew how much food was stolen by the kitchen staff. We knew of the unreported sexual assault on a female staff member. We knew the camp vehicle was taken "joyriding" after hours.

Chapter 2 touched on some of the problems that directors face in monitoring inappropriate activities that occur in their camps: the behavior is kept hidden, directors can be in only one place at a time, selective attention limits how much is perceived, and their expectations affect what they perceive. We cited the example of director Charles, who expected his camp to run smoothly, and assistant Brian, who expected staff to need close supervision. The example illustrated that personal judgment cannot be the sole factor in evaluating the culture of a camp. A director may believe that none of the negative influences we have described occur in camp. Unit leaders, though, may have quite a different perspective.

Relying solely on your own impressions can be a setup for long-term failure. But there are two measures you can take to confirm that your view matches that of other camp participants:

- Establish an effective feedback loop.

- Use systematic evaluation tools.

The Feedback Loop

All camp employees have valuable information about whether or not a season is successful. But just because a staff member has valuable feedback to give is no guarantee that it will reach the director's attention. Characteristics of the camp environment and the director influence the staff's decisions whether to share ideas or concerns.

The following suggestions will make feedback more likely to reach your ears.

- **Create a policy regarding comments, concerns, and suggestions, and implement it consistently.** Will there be an open-door policy? Is a chain of command to be followed? Is the suggestion box emptied every day? Formulate a specific protocol for acting on staff suggestions. Inform staff of the protocol, and follow through on its implementation.

- **Seek input from a variety of sources.** Do not rely simply on the judgment of favorite employees. Seek out feedback from the quiet, disgruntled, and "problem" employees as well.

- **Simplify the feedback process.** The more accessible you are to staff, the more likely you are to receive staff feedback. Requiring a written request three weeks in advance of a personal meeting is guaranteed to lessen staff enthusiasm.

Evaluation Tools

To supplement the informal feedback loop, a more systematic way of polling the staff is useful. Two common methods used by social scientists are the written survey and the personal interview. Both entail asking people carefully thought out questions, tallying the responses, and drawing conclusions based on the results. In devising formal evaluation tools, camp directors face the same challenge that social scientists do: the need to define problems clearly before gathering data. We especially lack clear definitions of appropriate and inappropriate sexual behavior.

To illustrate the importance of clear definitions, suppose you were asked to count the number of homeless people in your town. Before reading any further, define "homeless" to yourself. Now test your definition by asking yourself these questions: Does "homeless" mean only those who are living on the streets? What about those living in shelters? Does your definition include people who are living with relatives or friends because they cannot afford to rent an apartment? How about the family who have lost their home due to a fire and are living with others until their home is rebuilt? Does your definition of homelessness apply only if the major factor is lack of income, or does it apply to the loss of a home due to a disaster even though the person may still have supportive income? And what about the time factor? If a man has to live in a shelter for one month but otherwise has a place to reside, do you count him as homeless for the purpose of data collection? Consider also that ten people might come up with ten different definitions of "homeless."

This example illustrates the necessity of clearly defining a problem before data is collected. If the definition is broad, more cases will be reported. If the definition is narrow, fewer cases will be reported. Recall the camp board member who thought every sexual behavior was inappropriate and should result in sending the child or children home immediately. If that person prevails and such a broad policy is written, the camp data will reflect a larger number of inappropriate sexual acts than if the policy applies only to sexual acts involving coercion. Depending on which definition the board accepts, the number of cases requiring intervention by the camp director could be either large or small.

Lest this seem terribly complicated, let me reassure you that we've provided some guidance. In Chapter 8, we present two surveys you can use with staff and campers as part of an overall plan for camp safety. We also suggest some ways to conduct personal interviews.

Whether your formal evaluation tool is a written survey or personal interview, you need to ensure that you get honest responses. Participants should not think they risk repercussions for their honesty. Two strategies can minimize this concern:

- **Make your written survey anonymous.** You will receive more honest responses if participants are not required to give their name.

- **Clearly state the purpose of the evaluation.** It is not to seek out dissatisfied employees but to learn participants' different perceptions on camp safety.

I hope this chapter has given you some insight into how your own camp culture may contribute to inappropriate activities. If you confirm your personal observations by involving staff in an informal feedback loop and a more formal program of evaluation, you will be in a better position to offer a camp experience that is physically and psychologically safe.

*When relationship violence occurs, camp
directors must remember they are not
judges or therapists.*

4

Sexual Assault between Staff Members

How well I recall the first time a sexual assault was reported to me in a camp! Naturally I was concerned with the welfare of the victim, but I was also concerned with the reputation of the camp, not to mention my own reputation. How should I handle the incident? Had I somehow allowed it to occur? How would this reflect on my leadership? Would I lose my job? Would the media become involved? I was frantic!

I have learned much since then through my experience with clinical treatment and the legal system. I now recognize that reported incidents are only the tip of the iceberg. Most sexual assaults are never reported. A variety of physically violent behaviors can occur within relationships, and most of these, too, are never reported. Even without any physical contact, interpersonal encounters can be coercive, intimidating, threatening, and frightening overall. Camp directors should know that various combinations of these behaviors occur among staff but usually beneath the radar screen of our awareness.

The research presented in Chapter 2 showed how important relationships are in our lives. Ironically, relationships can also be the biggest source of stress. Warr and Payne (1982) asked a sample of adults what, if anything, had caused them emotional strain the prior day. The most frequent response was "family." Camp directors are well aware of the stress in their own close relationships. They also know that relationships can affect their staff for both good and bad. The stress created in close relationships can be a factor in assault and other coercive behaviors. During a camp season, it is probable that at least one staff member will find the behavior or attention of another staff member unwelcome, sexually intrusive, and/or harassing. Some behaviors will be so severe as to warrant immediate termination and possible police involvement.

One of the major points stressed in camp orientations is safety, and rightly so, as the safety of campers is a staff member's most important role. Federal law requires a safe working environment, and the American Camping Association's *Accreditation Standards for Camp Programs and Services* (1998) lists numerous hazards that must be attended to, from the storage of flammable materials to medication management at the health center. But although safety is a priority for the camping industry, sexual safety is a new concept for many camp administrators.

The camping industry is not alone in hesitating on this unfamiliar path. Schools, nursing homes, hospitals, mental health facilities, residential treatment facilities, the military—all are struggling to formulate effective, reasonable policies for sexual safety, mostly focused on acts of sexual harassment and sexual assault. All have found that creating such policies is fraught with complexity.

Stressed romantic relationships are at the root of many a sexual assault. It is thus important to recognize their presence in camps. In this chapter, we examine sexual assault in camp settings and recommend ways to cope when it occurs. But first we examine the research on general relationship violence, both physical and psychological, which describes certain triggers that play a role in sexual assault.

Unrealistic Expectations of Self-Control

Surveys of numerous workplace environments indicate that quite a number of employees are involved in liaisons with co-workers. A 1994 American Management Association poll (cited in Meyer, 1998) found that at least one-fourth of professional workers had been romantically involved with a colleague. Romance is no less likely in camps. Indeed, in my own experience, romantic relationships among camp staff are a noted aspect of camp life, probably involving more than a quarter of camp staff. Camp directors estimate that as many as 80 percent of their staff become involved in romantic relationships.

A vignette I commonly use in interviewing staff for camp positions focuses on romantic attraction:

> After working at camp for almost a month, you realize that another staff member finds you attractive and wants to start a relationship with you. The attraction is mutual—you, too, are interested. How would you handle this attraction? And how could you keep this camp romance from interfering with your job?

I pitched these questions in countless interviews, and not once did candidates doubt their ability to handle such a situation. All were quite confident that such an attraction would pose no obstacle to performing their job. They would say things like:

"I'm already in a relationship. I'm not going to camp to find a romantic partner."

"This is a job. If I were to find a person attractive, I would wait until camp was over before pursuing any type of relationship."

"I know myself. I would not allow a romantic relationship to happen."

The candidates could be quite vocal in assuring me they could manage themselves and their romantic emotions. But could they follow through? Using the past season as an example, by the end of the summer, approximately 50 percent of the staff were or had been involved in a camp relationship. Some "couples" had already broken up and were not speaking to each other. Two males went into the forest surrounding the camp to "duel" over a female. Two others announced their homosexuality and began to date. All in all, there was drama enough to make a soap opera appear tame.

We now know that humans think they have more control over themselves than they actually do. Recent findings in psychology and biology agree that we tend to overestimate how much control we have. In one experiment, gamblers engaged in rolling dice used more force when trying to roll high numbers than when trying to roll low numbers. The numbers actually rolled were random, but the participants acted as though they could influence the roll (Langer, 1975). In another study, most shoppers were favorably influenced by rebate offers when making purchases, but few ultimately sent in the form required to obtain the rebate (Tat, Cunningham, & Babakus, 1988). No doubt you have had this experience yourself.

Humans especially overestimate how they will manage themselves in a sexual situation. Study after study finds that many people who say they intend to use condoms during sexual activity fail to act on that intent in the "heat of the moment." By the same token, job candidates find it easy to assert perfect control over emotions and arousal when in the interview room but not so easy in the real world of camp. People tend to underpredict the strength of sexual desire and infatuation. The majority of my interviewees truly believed that relationships would not occur or would not affect their job performance. Although a few might have intended to use camp as a base for exploring their sexual freedom, most came to camp with the full intent of refraining from sex.

A common but unfortunate belief is that romantic relationships hinder the operation of a camp. In all fairness, there is a positive side to workplace romance. During the initial infatuation period, most individuals are in a state of elation and experience consistent contentment and happiness. This emotional combination often makes these individuals more resistant to stress, more energized, and more pleasant in the workplace.

In an example from a past season, a female staff member assisted the waterfront staff member she was romantically involved with to prepare a highly complicated obstacle course on a very humid day. Other staff balked at this task, but this female not only accepted the assignment with anticipation but also worked harder on it than any of her co-workers. She behaved this way not because she found deep satisfaction in the project but because she was able to assist her "partner." Thus we should not assume that romantic relationships are always detrimental to the workplace.

Dating Violence

Romantic relationships can be a source of pain, as many of us can attest. The giddy and energizing period of infatuation can dissipate into misunderstanding, hurt feelings, and, sadly, attempts at revenge. Many think of pain in relationships as associated with break-ups and separation. But the pain can stem from actual physical and psychological violence.

The following studies reveal the extent of physical violence in relationships:

- A 2000 study of 635 high school students showed that one-third, including both males and females, had experienced physical violence in dating relationships. Girls reported being punched or forced to engage in sexual activity more often, while boys reported more incidents of being pinched, slapped, scratched, and kicked. Less than 3 percent of victims reported this violence to an authority figure (Molidor, Tolman, & Kober, 2000).

- About 35 percent of women reported having been physically assaulted by a dating partner (DeKeseredy & Kelly, 1993).

- Between 15 and 25 percent of male college students engaged in physical and/or sexual aggression towards females (Wolfe, Wekerle, Reitzel-Jaffe, & Gough, 1995).

- National surveys indicate that more than 35 percent of both men and women inflict some form of physical aggression on their dating partners (White & Koss, 1992).

As you can see, both males and females initiate and become targets of physical aggression. These findings are just a tiny sampling of the research on physical abuse in relationships.

Psychological abuse can take many forms. The abusive partner may try to isolate the victim from friends and family, control the victim's actions, engage in coercive verbal abuse, and use threats and intimidation. Individuals who employ these techniques are attempting to fully possess another person. This description may "hit home" if you have been in such a relationship yourself; if not, you may find strange the idea of fully possessing another person. But I have yet to work with a camp director who could not recall at least one example of a camp romance that seemed "too possessive." Some of these relationships may have been dangerously dysfunctional.

Violence in relationships is usually hidden from authorities. Recall that less than 3 percent of high school students who had been victims of dating violence reported the incidents. Perhaps even more significant, about 50 percent of dating relationships do not end after a violent episode. Surveys have found that as many as three-quarters of women involved in violent dating relationships still plan on marrying their partner. No wonder directors learn so little about relationship violence occurring in their camps.

A Developmental Perspective

Knowing that romantic relationships are bound to form in camps and that some of them will become physically or psychologically violent, can we identify those people likely to commit violent acts? People often assume that sexual assaults are committed by aggressive individuals who are incapable of managing their emotions. If camp directors could just find a way to identify such individuals during the interview process, they could avoid hiring them and the camp would be a safe workplace.

Unfortunately, this is a fantasy. Although sexually aggressive individuals present a high risk for interpersonal violence, the majority of perpetrators do not fit this classification. In fact, most perpetrators of relationship violence have no outstanding characteristics that could be pinpointed in an interview. Some may not even be aware of their capacity for violence until placed in a specific environment conducive to such conduct. **Camp directors should give up the notion that they need only identify a culprit and deal with him or her accordingly.** Camp directors need to adopt a more comprehensive—and therefore more challenging—view of relationship violence to understand what leads to sexual assault. We begin with a look at differences in how boys and girls develop.

For the majority of boys and girls, romantic relationships begin during adolescence. Most adolescents experience at least one exclusive relationship lasting for several months to a year. As adolescents mature into young adults, romantic relationships take precedence over other relationships, though they do not appear to affect the levels of closeness with parents, siblings, and friends.

Due to their very different experiences in childhood, males and females typically enter romantic relationships with differing interpersonal skills. This difference can make romantic relationships rather tumultuous. The roots go back into childhood.

As early as eighteen months, but certainly between the ages of three and four, children begin to prefer to play with others of their own sex, a characteristic found throughout the world. Girls are the first to demonstrate this same-sex preference. The play style of these same-sex groupings is quite different. Males prefer active play with displays of dominance, while females prefer more cooperative and interpersonal interactions. According to research by Leaper (1994):

- Boys are more motivated toward power and dominance, whereas girls are more motivated to seek affiliation and closeness.

- Girls' groups tend to emphasize being able to read social situations with sensitivity and consideration. Girls are more likely than boys to use polite and indirect forms of influence that help to reduce conflict, such as requests and compromise, and girls tend to offer more open expressions of support than do boys.

- The activities and social interaction styles of boys' groups reflect their concern with competition and dominance. Their involvement in team sports provides a basis for establishing rank according to ability.

- Boys tend to use more domineering influence strategies such as demands, threats, and physical force, and they more often engage in competitive conflicts in same-sex interactions. In fact, this competitiveness may be even greater with friends than with non-friends. Even in friendly conversations, males tend to confront one another with challenges, mockery, and bravado (pp. 69–70).[*]

Due to self-selection into same-sex play groups, boys and girls grow up with different experiences of the world and learn different interpersonal skills. Girls practice skills of social sensitivity that enable them to achieve interpersonal closeness and intimacy. Males practice assertion and may be less prepared for the demands of intimate relationships that occur in adolescence and adulthood. They may even place females in positions of lower power and status in relationships. Such differences set the stage for misunderstandings, complications, and occasional dangers when intimate encounters occur.

Triggers for Relationship Violence

Relational stress can erupt into violence when certain triggers set them off. These are some of the common triggers:

- Rejection
- Jealousy
- Alcohol
- Misunderstandings
- Differing interests

Camp examples of these triggers are easy to recall. In one case, a female staff member became romantically and sexually involved with a male cook within days of starting her first camp experience. Three weeks later she found herself attracted to a male waterfront staff member. When she ended the relationship with the cook, he responded by subtly harassing the waterfront person. The latter became so concerned for his own safety as the end of the season approached that he left the job early.

One way to deal with jealousy and rejection is to evoke jealousy in a partner. A counselor who believed that her boyfriend had a sexual interest in another person began a series of flirtations with other male staff. She was known to parade these facts to the bewildered boyfriend.

Another common response to jealousy and rejection is to belittle perceived competitors. A male counselor spread a story around camp that another counselor had a very small penis—he supposedly knew this because males showered together in an open area.

---

[*]From C. Leaper, "Exploring the consequences of gender segregation on social relationships." In C. Leaper (Ed.), *Childhood gender segregation: Causes and consequences.* Copyright ©1994 by Jossey-Bass Publishers. Reprinted by permission of John Wiley & Sons, Inc.

The event that triggered this behavior was that a female that the perpetrator liked became romantically involved with the subject of the story.

When reacting in jealousy or against rejection, men tend to belittle the accomplishments and resources of a rival, such as his car, money, or social standing. Women tend to belittle a rival's physical appearance, such as her body shape, clothing, or hairstyle (Buss, 2000).

The use of alcohol can especially fan the flames of jealousy and rejection. By lowering a person's inhibitions, alcohol can lead a person to pursue harmful means to achieve revenge. Drinking alcohol can easily lead to physical violence in such scenarios.

Other triggers for interpersonal violence are misunderstandings and divergent interests. One partner may want to do this, while their partner wants to do that. Most couples settle their differences without resorting to aggression, but those who have not developed the needed interpersonal skills may fall back on threats, intimidation, and/or overt violence to get what they want. Do not assume that only your younger staff will have difficulty resolving disputes in their relationships. Older, presumably more mature staff members may also lack the interpersonal skills needed for non-violent dispute resolution.

Though we easily envision the dominant male forcing his needs onto the submissive female, research shows that females tend to try to control the situation just as males do. The striking difference is that females tend to use verbal means of control such as complaining or expressing anger. In his review of the literature, Felson (2002) concludes that wives use more controlling behavior than their husbands and that women with a high need for control are just as willing as males to use physical violence to get revenge. However, due to the characteristic size differences between the sexes, the violence is less likely to harm the targeted male.

When individuals lack the ability to maturely resolve an immediate critical event in their relationship, studies show that most of them react in one of three negative ways, any of which could trigger violence:

• Trying to control the behavior of another

All camp directors have seen new staff members use verbal threats to control the behavior of campers, such as, "If you don't quiet down, you'll go to bed early tonight." The threat of violence can also be used to ensure a victim's future cooperation. An example of this occurred when a male counselor verbally accosted his camp girlfriend whom he found talking to another male. He followed this up with several hours of silence in which he refused to respond to her protestations. He finally explained that this was "just a taste" of what would happen next time if she were found talking to another male.

• Trying to gain retribution, revenge, or justice

Our social interactions offer many possibilities for being offended or having our feelings hurt. Many of us simply accept such grievances and allow ourselves to forget, but others seek some form of payback. In the experience of many directors, payback comes in the form of camp pranks. On the surface camp pranks appear amusing and even clever, but their intent is to hurt or offend another person. One female unit leader found her bike—her inter-camp mode of transportation—submerged in the lake. This occurred shortly after a break-up with a male unit leader. Though the unit leader did not personally commit this act of theft and vandalism, he had arranged for some of his counselors to take care of the matter.

- ### Trying to protect one's self-image

By using violence, a person may demonstrate that he or she is powerful and worthy of respect.

In most cases of camp violence, the director, with some consideration, can see that the incident reflects one or more of these three motivating factors. It may be difficult to separate the factors from each other. In the example of the hurtful bicycle prank, the perpetrator was trying to get back at his girlfriend and also trying to fortify his image with his peers. A violent episode may involve all three factors.

So far in this chapter, we have gained insight into relationship violence, both physical and psychological, by examining it from several perspectives. We have seen that, from their early segregation into same-sex play groups, males and females develop different sets of interpersonal skills to rely upon when disagreements occur. We have seen the strong emotions of jealousy and rejection associated with relationship violence. Finally, we have seen that when couples disagree, disputes can lead to revenge, efforts at control, and/or protection of one's image, all of which can trigger violence.

The Roots of Sexual Assault

We now move from general relationship violence to one specific from of violence: sexual assault. This inclusive label subsumes many specific sexual acts, ranging in severity from unwanted touching (fondling) to violent physical harm. What all these acts have in common is that a person is subjected to unwelcome physical contact.

While sexual assault by a stranger may occur on camp property, the more realistic concern is sexual assault occurring between people who know each other. In fact, most cases of sexual assault take place within established relationships between friends, romantic partners, or passing acquaintances. Only rarely do they occur between individuals who had no prior contact. It is often difficult to evaluate the validity of an assault charge when those involved are in a relationship. A staff member sexually assaulted while returning from the laundry room by an unknown assailant is a clear example of criminal activity. When romantic relationships are involved, criminal intent is far less clear.

Acts of sexual assault imply an element of coercion. Because males are usually larger and stronger than females, females are most often the victims. This does not mean that females do not physically attack males, only that men rarely report these incidents. It is difficult for a female to intimidate a male if she is smaller, weighs less, and is less strong. Of course, a female might coerce a male into unwanted sexual behaviors, especially if she has legitimate power over him, as a female supervisor has over a male employee. Yet when speaking of forced sexual activity, we most often refer to the victim as female and the perpetrator as male.

Coercion is certainly an extreme way to engage another person in sexual activity, but it is one of a number of indirect ways in which both males and females elicit sex, including persuasion, deception, enhancement of self-presentation, and offering rewards. Individuals of both sexes devote a portion of their day to enhancing their appearance through exercise and/or the application of make-up. Males may elicit sex by treating a date to a very expensive meal, putting on their best behavior, and professing love that they do not actually feel. Greer and Buss (1994) found that the most successful tactic for engaging a female in sexual activity is to invest time and attention and profess love and commitment. According to Perper and Weis (1987), females express sexual interest through talking (laughing, complimenting, sexual talk), environmental signaling (seductive clothing, dancing, creating a "romantic atmosphere"), touching (holding hands, caressing), and kissing.

Note that in none of these examples is there a direct request for sexual activity. It would certainly be easier to ask a person directly, but the social norm is to employ less direct methods. As a result, much of the sexual activity in newly formed couples is initiated through indirect means. The very ambiguity of these indirect means often leads to miscommunication. Sexual signals can easily be misinterpreted, which is often the root cause of sexual assaults that occur in camp.

When combined with passion, sexual miscommunication is a problem waiting to happen. Sexual arousal affects the functioning of the human brain. It can interfere with judgment and self-control, not just lowering inhibitions against the use of coercion but also reducing awareness of a partner's reactions. During moments of passion, the long-term consequences of sex are minimized or out-and-out ignored.

Sexual assault between staff members most often occurs either when sexual cues are misinterpreted or when an existing romantic relationship undergoes stress. In a typical scenario, a male misinterprets a female's cues and even perceives her use of the word "no" as mere token resistance. He proceeds to make physical contact based on how he conceives their interaction. In another typical scenario, a male in a stressed romantic relationship attempts some form of retribution, control of his partner, and/or image-protection. The use of alcohol in either scenario likely makes the negative consequences even worse.

One wonders about the true extent of sexual coercion in camps when males and females who had few interactions as children are thrust together. Ill-equipped to communicate with the opposite sex, they must not only cope with their own sexual desires but also signal that interest and interpret the interest of others—often without verbal means. Biological differences in sexual arousal between males and females, described in Chapter 5, further complicate the picture. One shudders to think that all this is occurring on camp premises in an environment that naturally fosters intimacy.

Kennedy-Moore and Watson (1999) depict the confusing situation that our young people face:

[S]exual expression seems to involve a lot of fumbling around in the dark (physically and metaphorically). When we consider the complexity of cultural proscriptions, the multiplicity of interpersonal goals, the subtlety of sexual cues, the variety of relationship histories, and the fluidity of partners' perceptions and interpretations of sexual expressions, it seems miraculous that anyone ever establishes a mutually satisfying sexual relationship (p. 152).

Yet individuals go on to develop just such satisfying sexual relationships. As a relationship deepens, partners learn more about each other's likes and dislikes, rely less on cultural prohibitions, and become more able to talk productively about sex. If only camp directors could hire couples already involved in long-term committed relationships, the challenges in this chapter might be moot. But the reality of the camping industry is that directors must deal with the fallout from budding sexual relationships.

What to Do?

When incidents of sexual assault are reported, directors naturally want a set of clear instructions to swiftly resolve the problem. Unfortunately, such a set of instructions does not exist. Each incident has its own dynamics, and an approach that appears sensible in one situation may be foolish in another. The many variables that combine in sexually inappropriate activity work against trying to define a blanket intervention for all cases.

Chapter 8 provides a plan action to help prevent harmful sexual activity from occurring. But even the best prevention plan is no guarantee against incidents of sexual assault.

Instead of specific instructions, we offer a frame of mind that directors can maintain when faced with a report of sexual assault. If an incident occurs in your camp, this mindset will help you maintain a healthy perspective during those difficult hours following the initial report.

Note: A sexual assault committed by a supervisor against a supervisee is considered sexual harassment, which we cover in Chapter 5. Such an assault falls under the sexual harassment guidelines of the Equal Employment Opportunity Commission (EEOC), the federal agency established to deal with workplace discrimination. I recommend, though, that all camps approach a sexual assault as a possible case of sexual harassment. This offers not only a recognized legal model for intervention but also makes practical sense in coping with the aftereffects of an accusation.

---

1. Stay calm.

It does not help anybody if the camp director loses control in a critical situation. Many directors worry about the implications of a sexual assault instead of focusing on immediate action steps. In particular, camp directors who subscribe to the fallacies presented in Chapter 2—that camps should guarantee a safe experience, or that sexual activity can somehow be regulated out of camps—are at risk for making questionable decisions. These fallacies only compound the negative emotions surrounding such incidents and make rational decisions more difficult.

Consider the camp director who firmly believes that camps should offer a safe environment. He or she will experience fear and guilt in addition to the anxiety that violent incidents evoke. It would be wonderful if a camp could guarantee safety, but it simply cannot. Of course, if a director has been negligent in regard to participant safety, he or she will have to deal with the consequences. But if a director has done all that could be done to make the environment safe, guilt and anxiety cause needless suffering and interfere with reasonable interventions.

2. Give the victim partial control of the situation.

Sexual assault must be treated as the crime that it is, but the victim should be allowed some choice in how to proceed. The most important choice a victim can make is whether or not to call the police. This contact initiates the involvement of the legal system, which will investigate and prosecute to determine guilt or innocence. The victim may want to talk to family members before deciding on police involvement. This is acceptable, but ultimately it must be the victim's choice.

It is *not* the victim's choice to determine whether the alleged offender should be fired or receive some other form of punishment. I have heard of camps that granted this right to a victim, but this is inappropriate. An accusation against a person does not necessarily equate with actual guilt, nor does an accusation mean that the victim will see the case through the judicial system. In my experience in the legal system with those charged with sexual offenses, I grew accustomed to accused males having their charges dropped after a preliminary hearing and victims recanting their stories even though they initially made serious charges.

With regard to police investigation, consider the following:

- Every state has in place a mandatory reporting protocol for child abuse. If the victimized staff member is under the age of eighteen, you may be obligated to report this to a youth protective agency.

- Some camps have a policy requiring police to investigate all cases of sexual assault even if the victim declines such involvement. This is done not so much for the protection of the victim but rather to have a written record on file for the camp's own legal security. The downside to mandating police investigation is that victims may be reluctant to report less severe incidents to the administration, knowing they will have to speak to police.

I recommended that directors contact their local police and youth protective agency to ascertain their requirements for handling incidents of sexual assault.

3. Do not act as a judge.

It is difficult to be impartial when a victim tearfully describes a sexual assault. One is naturally inclined to have sympathy for the victim and disdain for the alleged attacker. We say "alleged" because, as we have seen, sexual assault results from misperception or misinterpretation of subtle sexual cues between two people in a relationship. Although we may be tempted to slip into polarized thinking with an easily identified victim and villain, in reality we do not know the underlying dynamics that preceded the assault.

The good news is that camp directors are not called upon to decide guilt or innocence. Indeed, no camp director should try. This is a judgment that the legal system undertakes. For camp directors to try to secure evidence that reaches the criminal courts' standard of "beyond a reasonable doubt" is ill-advised no matter how well-intentioned. **The duty of the director is to create a safe environment and make all efforts to prevent similar assaults.** Your legal obligation as an employer is to establish and maintain a workplace free of harassment, and the relevant question is what you can do to keep similar events from happening in the future. This obligation is vastly different from judging guilt or innocence.

If a director is not to determine guilt or innocence, how can a director act on an accusation of assault? An obvious first step is to take note of any evidence. Some assaults show physical evidence of violence such as bruises and torn clothing or occur in the presence of witnesses. Such obvious physical harm of another camp participant may be grounds for immediate termination under your camp safety policy, even if the victim declines police involvement. But most assaults that occur in camp will show no evidence of physical harm.

For example, two staff members go to a bar on their night off and return slightly intoxicated. The man begins to make sexual advances upon the female, groping her and using obscene language. She quickly leaves and reports the incident to her supervisor. This male's behavior is certainly against the law. How does the director respond? First, the director does not take sides or assign blame. He offers the female an opportunity to contact the police. It is up to the victim to initiate legal proceedings. If she does, the courts will decide guilt or innocence. The male will likely be shocked, scared, and/or belligerent. But unless the incident is especially flagrant and confirmed by evidence, firing the male may have unintended consequences.

The dilemma is how to weigh the alleged victim's welfare and the camp's reputation against the consequences of a wrongful termination. It is here that the director must investigate with the sole purpose of collecting information that will lead to creating a harassment-free environment. If the male in question poses too much risk to the camp for future harassment charges, the director may decide to terminate his employment. The question is not so much whether the accused did or did not perform an assault, but whether he poses too much risk for similar behavior in the future. The frequency of the act, the severity of the act, and whether harm was intentional or unintentional—all these factors play a role in deciding whether to terminate, discipline, or do nothing.

Incidentally, the victim need not be completely satisfied with the outcome of the director's investigation. If she presses charges, the legal system will determine guilt or innocence and appropriate punishment. A camp director must be reasonable, effective, and expedient in dealing with the alleged sexual assault. The director's intervention will be judged on these factors, not on how satisfied the victim is with the consequences for the offender.

The director must also deal with the effect of a termination on other staff, if not on the entire camp. Each person will have an opinion on what form of justice is appropriate, so any decision a director makes is bound to offend someone. Staff may have trouble grasping that it is not the director's role to administer justice in sexual assault cases. The director's role is to create a safer environment for all participants, and this can include making changes based on the details of the assault case. The best defense is to be certain that all employees understand this policy, a point we emphasize in Chapter 8.

4. Do not act as a therapist.

The camp director is not responsible for solving relationship problems. The complexities of a relationship, especially one exhibiting violence, are such that a well-intentioned suggestion may cause more harm than good. Camp directors tend to be empathic individuals, but most are not trained social workers or therapists. A director can offer empathy, support, and a safe environment in which to discuss an incident of physical violence, but it is not appropriate for the director to offer counseling. Professional therapy may be called for, and a director should make a list of local resources available to participants in the incident.

5. Treat those involved as employees first.

This should be your mindset no matter what relationship the staff have with camp administrators and amongst themselves. Two statements I hear in just about every sexual assault case are:

"He didn't mean it."

"She's not telling the truth" or "she's exaggerating."

These statements are usually made by family and friends of the accused. But how do they know? The closer we are to people, the more difficult it can be to determine motives in an alleged sexual offense.

It is not uncommon for empathic camp professionals to become embroiled in the relationship turmoil of their staff members. One program director I worked with had a group of female staff meet in her cabin each night to discuss the ups and downs of their camp relationships. Is this a wise thing for a director to do? A professional boundary is essential. It is too easy to allow our knowledge about the personal lives of staff to interfere with our better judgment. A director may be intent on soothing negative emotions in a known couple when, in actuality, the male's behavior constitutes sexual harassment. Or a director may know a staff member so well as to be incapable of finding fault when that person is accused of sexual assault.

More and more businesses have given up attempting to restrict relationships between employees. They only intervene in cases of unwanted sexual contact, harassment, or when a romantic relationship interferes with job performance. I think that camps would be wise to follow these same guidelines. **We should think of our staff as employees and co-workers before we think about them as they often consider themselves, as romantic partners or friends.**

I would not be surprised if at least some readers balk at this recommendation. After all, camp people have a reputation for being outgoing and sociable. It is in our nature to seek personal relationships with our staff. To be asked to refrain from involvement in their lives seems to run counter to what we are all about.

The point is we do not need to become involved in *all* aspects of our staff's lives. If a staff member has a pressing question about sex, we need not turn the person away, but we should refrain from probing into this aspect of their being. We will certainly intervene when unwanted physical contact occurs, when sexual harassment is occurring or possibly occurring, and when sexual activity affects job performance or the general camp environment. But we are needlessly complicating our professional lives if we become involved in the romantic and sexual relationships of our staff.

*Camps can take a proactive approach to
unwelcome, offensive sexual behavior.*

5

Sexual Harassment

A female counselor lost one of her contact lenses. As a temporary remedy, she put on a pair of glasses that she kept for just such a situation. This was the first time any of her co-workers and campers had seen her wearing frames. At the camp game show that night, she walked to the stage to participate in the competition. Within seconds of stepping onto the platform, she heard a chorus of older male campers begin to chant in unison "glasses, glasses…." Other campers joined in, and soon the entire auditorium was filled with the voices of children and staff loudly chanting the word. The counselor controlled herself just long enough to leave the building before she burst into tears. A co-worker who came out to comfort her told her that the unit that started the chant was led by the male who, until two days prior, had been the victim's romantic interest in camp. The counselor immediately approached the director to press a "sexual harassment" charge against her former boyfriend for his leadership in the taunting.

In another incident, two female kitchen staff became uncomfortable when a delivery truck driver whistled at them as he unloaded an order of milk. The women informed the camp director of this unwanted attention. The camp director listened to them and said he intended to speak to the driver on his next delivery, but other problems arose that morning and prevented him from completing the task. Again the driver whistled at the females. Afterward, a well-intentioned program director told the women to inform the camp director that they were being sexually harassed and that he had to solve this problem or face legal consequences.

In a final example, a female camp counselor found herself receiving unwanted romantic attention from a male counselor. When she turned down his offer of a date, she had to cope with his retribution. This male had his whole cabin of boys "blow kisses" in her direction when they saw her. One of his campers, dressed in female clothing, portrayed her in a highly suggestive talent show skit. Finally, her underwear was stolen and found atop the flagpole. Though attempting to hide her embarrassment, the victim of these pranks was deeply uncomfortable with the entire chain of events. She told her friends of her discomfort, but she did not share her feelings with camp administration.

These vignettes portray behaviors that some might label sexual harassment. Do they really meet recognized standards for sexual harassment? This is an important question, because any employer who has fifteen or more employees, which most camps do, is required to follow federal guidelines for preventing and intervening in cases of sexual harassment. The director's action will be guided by the legal definition of sexual harassment and must follow federal guidelines.

Legal Definitions of Harassment

Just this past summer in my own camp, two female employees made an accusation of harassment against a co-worker. Both were wrong. I have no doubt that they felt harassed, but their claims did not even come close to meeting the federal criteria of sexual harassment. Like the female in the first example, the women in my camp had experienced teasing. They wanted it stopped and the responsible party punished. An incident of teasing, however, does not equate with sexual harassment.

Although sexual harassment certainly occurs in camps, it is rarely reported, and I could find no evidence of camp incidents that went through the legal system. But we can learn from a non-camp example that made its way to court.

A female welder was employed in a mostly male shipyard company. Her co-workers subjected her to nude photographs posted in places where she was bound to come across them, such as her toolbox. The men referred to her as "baby" and "sugar" continuously. They wrote sexual graffiti about her throughout the plant and made comments to her about her body and her sex life. The shipyard employer was found guilty of not intervening in ongoing sexual harassment. The resulting heavy financial penalty was quite a wake-up call for the company.

No camp wants a similar wake-up call. The problem is, charges of sexual harassment are often made indiscriminately while sufferers of truly unlawful harassment remain silent. How does a camp director recognize authentic harassment when it occurs?

According to the Equal Employment Opportunity Commission (EEOC), unlawful harassment is defined as **behavior that unreasonably interferes with an individual's work performance or creates an intimidating, hostile, or offensive working environment. This harassment must be based upon race, skin color, national origin, age, gender, religion, or disability.** These are federally protected groups. Local and state laws may recognize additional protected groups, for example, based on sexual orientation.

Most camps have wisely established a blanket harassment policy. This safeguards not just the protected groups but all camp participants against harassment. If all camp participants are protected from harassment—whether in an officially protected group or not—potential problems are averted.

Criteria of Sexual Harassment

Since our focus here is on behavior of a sexual nature, let us examine what constitutes unlawful sexual harassment.

- The behavior must be unwelcome.

- The behavior would be found offensive by a reasonable person.

- The behavior continues after the person engaging in the behavior has been informed that it is unwelcome.

- The behavior interferes with the ability of the victim to perform his or her job.

To charge unlawful sexual harassment, *all* of these criteria must be met unless the perpetrator is a supervisor, in which case even *one* event is enough to warrant harassment charges.

In regard to the second criterion, behavior found offensive by a reasonable person, the courts have introduced the concept of a "reasonable woman" rather than a "reasonable person" in examining the details of a case. This is quite important, because males may be far less offended than females by conduct of a sexual nature. The courts have thus recognized the need to examine sexual conduct in light of what a female, not a male, might find offensive. This seemingly small modification has and will continue to have a dramatic impact on future harassment hearings.

Note that one incident is rarely sufficient to classify as unlawful sexual harassment unless it occurs within a supervisory relationship. Also, behavior need not be explicitly sexual to be considered sexual harassment. Any behavior that demeans or ridicules persons of one sex can be considered sexual harassment.

Federal law does not prohibit simple teasing and isolated incidents that are not extremely serious. Another case shows what is meant by "extremely serious" behavior. Three female workers in a construction site were continuously subjected to verbal sexual abuse. Male co-workers made frequent requests for oral sex, exposed themselves, grabbed the females against their will, and exhibited pornography. Such conduct was rightfully found to interfere with the ability of the women to complete their job responsibilities.

Camp Examples Revisited

In light of the legal criteria of sexual harassment, we return to the opening vignettes.

What about the counselor who was humiliated for wearing glasses? According to the legal criteria, her case qualifies as simple teasing and does constitute unlawful harassment. The fact that she found the teasing unpleasant and even offensive does not necessarily qualify the behavior as sexual harassment.

What about the kitchen workers subjected to whistling? The driver's whistling does not yet qualify as unlawful harassment. Although the whistling was unwelcome, and might be found offensive by a reasonable woman, it did not interfere with the kitchen workers' ability to complete their job. Further, the offender was never told to stop his behavior. It is doubtful that any court would find this camp negligent for two incidents of whistling. But if it continued and caused increasing discomfort for the females, it could be considered unlawful harassment. The camp director should ask the driver to stop the whistling and should monitor to see if the driver complies with the request.

This case illustrates an important point: Offenders can include not just supervisors and co-workers but even outside agents who do business with the company. The driver worked for an outside vendor who had legitimate business with the camp and regularly entered the property to deliver their wares. Even such an outside agent falls within the employer's responsibility to prevent and intervene in employee harassment.

The third example, the counselor belittled by campers led by her former boyfriend, is in many ways the most tragic. The victim was indeed disturbed by the vengeful activity of the scorned suitor. Any reasonable woman would have found the behavior offensive, especially the sexually suggestive skit. The behavior likely interfered with the counselor's ability to perform her job. Unfortunately, she did not report the incidents to the camp director, nor did she tell the former boyfriend that she wanted the behaviors to stop. A case could easily have been made that this man's behavior was unlawful harassment, and an intervention should have occurred.

Forms of Sexual Harassment

Federal law recognizes two forms of sexual harassment: quid pro quo and hostile work environment. We address quid pro quo (Latin for "this for that") first since it is less common than hostile environment harassment. However, both could occur in your camp setting simultaneously.

Quid Pro Quo

With the quid pro quo form of harassment, a person in authority demands sexual favors from a subordinate in exchange for a promotion, a raise, additional job opportunities, or simply being able to keep a job. An employee who does not comply with a supervisor's request may be demoted, transferred, negatively evaluated, blocked in a promotion attempt, or even fired. Businesses can be found liable for this form of harassment even if the administration has no awareness of the supervisor's behavior. This is important, because even if a camp director has absolutely no knowledge of a supervisor demanding sexual favors of an employee, the camp can still be held responsible for allowing harassment to occur.

Many corporations refrain from intervening in romantic relationships between co-workers if they have no negative effect on job performance. Interfering in employee relationships goes against our right of privacy, and many human resources administrators agree that the legal system would frown on this as well. It's a different story, however, when the romantic relationship is between a supervisor and a direct report. Companies agree that such a situation requires management intervention.

Supervisor-subordinate relationships have the most potential for workplace harm. It is nearly impossible in such situations to make organizational decisions free of personal considerations. Other employees will no doubt claim favoritism in day-to-day practice. By far the biggest concern, though, is what happens if there is a break-up. A person who supervises someone with whom he or she was once romantically involved must navigate through a minefield of negative emotions. With the potential for hurt, anger, desire for retribution, and myriad other painful emotions, the chances of these two people working well together are almost impossible. The chances for quid pro quo harassment, or at least a perception of it, are greatly multiplied.

For all these reasons, many businesses strictly forbid relationships between supervisors and their direct reports. If a relationship does develop, one or both employees may be asked to leave or to take another job assignment so that they are no longer supervisor and supervisee. If anyone is demoted, it is usually the supervisor.

I endorse this as a policy for camps. We cannot prevent romantic relationships, and to try to break them up would violate basic rights, but some relationships clearly have too much potential for damage. Staff should be told, before they come to camp, that if a romantic relationship occurs between individuals with unequal power, one person will have to leave or assume another camp position.

For example, one camp director asked a male program director to give up his position when it was learned that he was romantically involved with a female counselor. The program director quit instead of accepting a kitchen position. This was not an easy decision for the camp director, but it was justified and appropriate. The program director was well aware of the policy before he accepted the position.

Hostile Work Environment

Hostile work environment harassment is much more common than quid pro quo harassment. A hostile work environment exits when the workplace is intimidating or offensive. Its victims are not threatened with termination or some other menace to their career. Instead, they are barraged with sexually offensive behaviors or remarks. The underlying message is that a person can stay at the job as long as he or she wishes but will have to put up with these behaviors.

The list of unwelcome and offensive behaviors would be quite lengthy. The most common are:

- Telling sexual jokes.
- Sexual innuendos.
- Discussing sexual activities.
- Commenting on a person's body or sex life.
- Unnecessary touching.
- Computer games that depict sexual situations.
- Displays of pornography.
- Whistling and catcalls.
- Gifts of a sexual nature.
- Leering.
- Lewd or threatening letters.
- Sexual gestures.
- Pressure for dates.
- Sabotaging a co-worker's work.
- Sexist jokes and cartoons.
- Hostile put-downs of females.

To qualify as hostile environment harassment, the offensive behavior must be frequent, ongoing, repetitive, and part of an overall pattern. In contrast, welcome sexual banter and sexual playfulness are not considered harmful or derogatory.

Every camp director with whom I have consulted tells of at least one incident they witnessed that could have been considered sexual harassment. Since nobody came forward to complain, however, these incidents were never investigated. Swimming areas were a common problem area. Many camps have separate swim times for males and females, but how typical is it for males to stay close by and watch the females? A female program director described the males' behavior as "leering." Another common instance was the use of sexually suggestive material in talent shows or campfires that may have offended participants. Yet another instance was when a camp director would tell his female staff that they "look nice," a comment that some found unwelcome.

Further complicating the camp's sexual harassment policy is the possibility of third-party harassment. Third-party harassment occurs when a behavior is unwelcome to an observer even if it is acceptable to the individuals directly involved. For example, in a swimming incident, no female counseling or waterfront staff complained about males watching them during their swim period. However, a female cook who observed the males' behavior expressed her discomfort even though she was not part of the activity. In her opinion, the males' behavior was offensive and thus required intervention by the director.

You may have noted that in our examples, all the victims were females. This is no coincidence, as research confirms that more than 40 percent of females are the victims of some form of sexual harassment during their careers. Men also can be victims of sexual harassment, but the number of incidents is far less than for females. In addition, female victims of harassment appear to suffer more severe outcomes. Female victims are more likely than male victims to transfer to another part of an agency, to quit the job, or to lose the job. Surveys show that the majority of sexual harassment incidents are never reported—the victim either suffers in silence or leaves the place of employment.

I have no doubt that females are subjected to sexual harassment in camp settings, but most of this harassment is not severe or pervasive enough to stand up to legal definitions in court. As our examples show, harassment in camp is much more subtle. Because it is not severe enough to command immediate attention, camp directors tend to downplay its harmful effects, but they are making a mistake. Sexual harassment affects not just the victim but the workplace as well. An employee who is angry, scared, or confused cannot give him- or herself fully to the job. Tolerating apparently subtle harassment can encourage more overt harassment and create an overall hostile work environment.

Although somewhere in the history of the camping industry a supervisor may have threatened an employee with repercussions for withholding sexual activity, or a camp may have been so heavily sexist that female staff found it intolerable, most incidents of harassment in camp are more subtle, as our examples show.

Effects of Harassment

On Individual Employees
- Embarrassment
- Fear
- Self-consciousness about the incidents
- Change of daily routines to avoid the harassment

On the Organization
- Increased absenteeism
- Lower productivity
- Increased staff turnover
- Decline of morale in the general workplace
- Loss of respect for management
- Damage to the reputation of the organization
- Financial costs, especially those incurred through legal interventions

Motives for Harassment in Camps

Many people assume that sexual harassment is caused by individuals with a distaste—if not outright hatred—for females. I have definitely encountered males in camps who had such a mindset about their female co-workers and supervisors. One male was the most gregarious and well-mannered gentlemen you could hope to meet, at least in the presence of other males. The female staff, however, reported that he was abrupt, rude, and condescending to them. He displayed this behavior with all females and used graphic, strikingly vulgar vocabulary in describing women. His camp stay came to an abrupt end due to an incident at the waterfront. The male waterfront director had to leave for a family emergency, and a female was promoted to take his place. On the first day of her duty in the new position, the male in question balked at her requests, cursed at her, and actually walked off the dock, even though her requests were the same as the male waterfront director would have made.

Although cases like this occur, I believe—and am supported by the research literature—that such indiscriminate disregard for females is not the cause of most sexual harassment in the workplace, especially in camps. Three other factors are more often implicated in sexual harassment:

- ## Maintaining male dominance

One of the most accepted causal theories is that males use sexual harassment to maintain their dominant status and power in society and to keep females in a lesser position. They see women's work as less valuable, and indeed society still rewards women's work less than men's. Despite dramatic advances in the status of women in the United Sates, females still face a "glass ceiling" in their career aspirations, make less than males in the same positions, and still perform the majority of housework in two-wage-earner families.

Add to this the fact that most sexual harassment cases are brought by women against male supervisors or against abusive, offensive male-dominated workplaces. It is not too difficult to see that women still maintain a less regarded status in society. This is not a contemporary anomaly but an outgrowth of centuries of similar treatment.

- ## Retribution

Recall the examples that began this chapter. In two of these, the females were dealing with the unwanted effects of a camp relationship: In one example, the ending of a relationship prompted the male to initiate a group taunt focused on his former girlfriend. In another, the male was seeking revenge because his romantic overtures had been turned down. In Chapter 4 we said that jealousy and rejection are common triggers for relationship violence. They are also common triggers for harassing behaviors and payback is a likely response.

- ## Differences in sexuality

The most common cause of sexual harassment has to do with differences in sexuality between males and females. Males have evolved to read sexual interest in even the most innocuous events. They tend to disregard female protestations as lacking sincerity, and, unless challenged, will continue to use sexualized behaviors in a belief that they will at one point pay off. Because this causal factor implicates all males, we need to understand better the differences between male and female sexuality. A number of research studies shed light on this matter.

A Research Perspective

We know that the brains of males and females develop differently due to the influence of hormones on the fetus. Although the brains of the two sexes are similar, differences in development affect their sexuality. Research shows marked differences in male and female response to sexual situations (see, for example, Blum, 1997; Pinker, 1997; Buss, 2003).

We begin with one of the least controversial differences between males and females: men's biological response to visual stimuli. Men are more quickly aroused by visual sexual stimuli than females. "The male of the human species is aroused by the sight of nude women, not only in the flesh but in movies, photographs, drawings, postcards, dolls, and bit-mapped cathode-ray-tube displays" (Pinker, 1997, p. 471–472). The male response to visual displays has generated a multi-billion-dollar pornography industry. The history of art testifies to the male fascination with the nude female figure. Even primitive drawings depict female nudity.

Females do not appear to respond to male nudity in the same way that males respond to female nudity. The Kinsey Institute once showed a group of men and women a series of drawings and photographs of nude males or females (Blum, 1997). Researchers found that 54 percent of the men but only 12 percent of the women were aroused by the display.

In a camp-related example, one director had to forbid male staff and campers from nearing the swimming area when the females had their private swim time. Small groups of males would cluster at the top of a hill to watch and freely comment upon the females' bodies. Not so easily dissuaded, the male staff made a small clearing in the forest so that they could continue their observations from a hidden spot. The camp director did not find out about this until the concluding week of the season. Notably, there was no problem with females arranging to observe male swimmers in secret.

Not only are men more aroused by visual stimuli, they also become aroused more quickly than females and become aroused to more varied stimuli. Studies with animals have demonstrated that males of many species attempt to initiate sexual contact with objects that have only a vague resemblance to females of the same species—including females that have been stuffed and mounted! Research with humans tells a similar story. In one study, researchers played audiotapes of conversations for both male and female college students. Some of the conversations were purposely sexual, and others dealt with mundane topics such choosing one major over another. Most of the research participants found the erotic conversations sexually stimulating, but only males found the mundane topics sexually stimulating. Indeed, many of the men exhibited more physiological arousal to the mundane conversations than females did to the erotic conversations. The researchers observed that, "In humans, the male system seems so jittery with sexual readiness that just about anything—high-heeled shoes, a smile, a friendly conversation—will produce a sexual response" (Blum, 1997, p. 228).[*]

Males are far more likely to perceive a neutral event as sexual. Even the most neutral dialogue between a male and a female may be a source of sexual fantasy for the male. For example, a female staff member asks a male staff member to help carry some tents back to the equipment shed. The male may consider this some sort of hidden sexual invitation, while the female was simply asking for help and nothing more. In my clinical experience, I have seen males mistakenly sexualize even the most innocuous events, including a mere smile or "thank you" on the part of a female. Many males use such small incidents to create an elaborate fantasy of sexual encounter without bothering to see if the female has a mutual interest. A man may go on to approach a female as though she were just as interested in a sexual escapade as he.

Research confirms that males tend to overestimate females' interest in sex, often assuming that females have just as much interest as they themselves do (Felson, 2002). Young males may enter sexual relationships without an appreciation of the importance that females attach to sex. Since this is unlikely to be a subject of conversation in initial contacts with a potential partner, they must attempt to interpret subtle cues to determine the female's sexual interest.

Working against clear communication of sexual interest is the social norm that females should not appear too interested. Research has found that many women initially say "no" to sexual activity when they truly desire it. The phrase "token resistance" has been created to describe such a response. Studies show that a majority of females report initially declining sexual advances when they were in fact very interested or at least possibly interested. Females may use token resistance to express ambivalence, to increase their perceived worth by not giving in too easily, or to preserve a good reputation. For their part, males expect token resistance in initial sexual encounters and devote much effort to overcoming it. They often perceive token resistance as lacking sincerity, so they use such means as declarations of love, gift giving, or coercion to obtain the object of their desire. Although in legal terms "no" means "no," men perceive that, in psychological terms, "no" can mean "no" or "yes" or "maybe."

Men's view of sexual liaisons provides another contrast with women. Buss (2003) used written surveys to ask male and female participants if they would have sex with a person they had known for at least five years, for two years, for a month, or for a week. Most women would not even consider having sex with a person unless they had known each other for at least several months, whereas males would have sexual contact based on a week's acquaintance. In fact, some males would have sexual contact based on an hour's acquaintance.

In an intriguing psychological study, Clark & Hatfield (1989) hired attractive males and females to approach strangers on a busy college campus. These individuals were trained to say to the stranger, "I have been noticing you around campus. I find you very attractive." They would then ask one of three questions:

1. "Would you go out with me tonight?"

2. "Would you come over to my apartment tonight?"

3. "Would you go to bed with me tonight?

To the first question, about half of both males and females consented to a date. But from this similarity of response, their answers to the second and third questions diverged quite strikingly. Would it surprise you to find that men were much more willing than women to accept the latter two invitations? Only 6 percent of the females consented to go to the person's apartment, but 69 percent of the males consented. None of the females agreed to have sex, but 75 percent of the males agreed.

Finally, men are often persistent and undaunted in their sexual quests. One sexual "payoff" can compensate for an untold number of failures. A male staff member who leers at females and makes suggestive gestures is unlikely to be found sexually appealing. But if even one female engages in sexual activity with him, this will be reinforcement enough for him to continue the behavior despite the many failures that preceded this conquest.

Research and experience both predict that males are more diligent in seeking sexual encounters—even with several females consecutively. Many camp directors I work with complain about male staff exploiting females for their own sexual needs, even though their behavior is not illegal. Of course, some females also seek numerous sexual exploits, but they are in the minority compared to males. Says Blum (1997), "The boundaries between genders are naturally quite blurred. There are few things that only males or only females can do. That, however, is not the same as saying that there are few things that only males or only females are likely to do" (p. 279).[†]

Understanding the differences in male and female sexuality, we can better see that most harassment occurring in camps is an extension of men's persistent attempts to engage in activities that may result in sex, including disregarding the protests of the targeted females. A final example illustrates this point. Pam, a female unit leader, found a

---

gift from a secret admirer in her unit's mailbox. Every other day for two weeks she would find another small item—usually something made in arts and crafts. In a talk with the activity instructor, Pam learned the identity of the secret admirer. She thanked the admirer for the gifts but clearly told him that she was not interested in a romantic relationship. The male was not dissuaded, however. He continued to leave gifts, tracked her down for conversation during her time off, offered to teach her how to swim, and performed a ballad dedicated to her at a talent show. Pam became increasingly concerned with this attention. Although she did not consider the male's behavior as sexual harassment, she called it "creepy" and "uncomfortable." From an objective standpoint, his behaviors certainly crossed the boundary between acceptable and unacceptable. If he were told to stop but continued, the camp director could well be dealing with unlawful activity.

What to Do?

We have said that sexual harassment can be motivated by a need to assert male dominance and a desire to get even for being rejected or causing jealousy. Both of these motivations include an intent to harm females. Ironically, the third motivation—men's persistence in unwelcome advances toward females—intends no harm but is likely to be the most prevalent problem in camps.

In Chapter 4, we urged you not to play judge or therapist with incidents of sexual assault. A camp director must deal with the individuals as employees and co-workers, disregarding their relationship status. This applies to incidents of sexual harassment as well. However, there is a qualification. As cases are heard in the legal system, the laws regarding sexual harassment continue to be refined. Even Supreme Court justices have expressed legitimate differences of opinion on the subject. Thus you should not expect staff members to fully comprehend the issues.

Female staff may be uncertain whether bothersome day-to-day interactions could be defined as sexually harassing, so you need to be open to exploring such questions. The intent should not be to offer counseling but to listen carefully to discern if a particular behavior points to sexual harassment.

Male administrators would be wise to designate a certain female to receive training in harassment recognition and intervention in case women feel uncomfortable discussing such issues with a male. This woman can act as a gatekeeper, referring more serious cases to the director. For information on trainings and workshops, contact your local Equal Employment Opportunity Commission (EEOC). The American Camping Association also offers relevant materials.

As a general rule, if another person's behavior is unwelcome, offensive, and can be construed as sexual harassment (see the list of possible infractions on page 72), the director must investigate. This may be the first time a person's behavior was reported, but the behavior could have been occurring for some time. Also, a director's failure to intervene will cast a negative light on the camp in the unlikely event that the case goes to court.

The general approach to investigating and intervening in sexual harassment is the same as that recommended in Chapter 4 in cases of sexual assault:

- The director's duty is to create a safe environment and make all efforts to prevent harassment. The legal obligation of an employer is to establish and maintain a workplace free of harassment.

- The victim need not be satisfied with the outcome of an investigation. A camp director must be reasonable and effective in dealing with the alleged situation. A camp director's response to an accusation of sexual harassment will be judged on the basis of the reasonableness, effectiveness, and expediency of the investigation and intervention.

- The goal of the intervention is not punishment, although this can be an outcome, but to prevent future harassment.

- Staff should recognize that the administration takes personnel problems seriously. All complaints are investigated in a timely fashion and with the best interests of everyone in mind.

Interventions to Stop Harassment

Following are elements of the process recommended by the EEOC to track and resolve harassment cases (Wagner, 1992).

Victim-Initiated Notices and Warnings

The victim can take action to document and try to stop harassment through the following system of notices and warnings:

1. The victim gives notice to the offender that a specific behavior is unwelcome. If the offending person is the supervisor, the victim can give notice through a recognized third party such as a human resources officer.

2. *Optional, but recommended:* The victim gives a stronger warning and notice that she will inform authorities if the behavior continues.

3. *Optional, but recommended:* The victim issues a written warning.

4. The victim makes an informal harassment inquiry. This is the point at which camp directors often become involved.

Director's Informal Inquiry

Any expression of concern over possible harassment must be investigated. Such an investigation may not turn up harassment, but camp administration is legally obligated to initiate the process and make an independent judgment.

The initial investigation is informal, consisting simply of asking questions of each side and talking to any witnesses to the incident. Besides the who what where and how questions, some other relevant questions are:

- What is the parties' relationship? Did they know each other before working at the camp?
- Have prior allegations been raised by one party against the other?
- Did their supervisors notice anything to support the claims of either party?
- Was the conduct an isolated incident or a series of occurrences?
- Was the behavior meant to be taken seriously or meant as a joke?
- Would the conduct be found offensive by a reasonable woman?
- Could there be an ulterior motive for the victim's accusation?

The investigation should occur as soon as possible, and all aspects should be documented in a written record. Confidentiality for the accused and accuser should be maintained if at all possible. If this informal inquiry finds evidence of unlawful harassment, the director must take action to try to stop the harassment.

- In mundane violations such as males leering at females in the swimming area, it may be sufficient to publish a policy saying that such behavior is unwelcome and to follow up with monitoring to ensure compliance.

- In the case of less severe male-female harassment, the director could simply ask the employee if she would like to solve the problem on her own, discuss a plan, and follow up in a week or two.

- The director can select from a range of options to discipline the offender according to the gravity of the offense. These include asking for an apology, reviewing camp policy on harassment, education, mediation, counseling, written warning, suspension, transfer, and termination.

- If the harassment involved physical contact or was particularly serious, the police may be called if the victim so desires.

If the informal inquiry finds no evidence of unlawful harassment, this is reported to the victim. The victim then has at least three options:

1. If the victim is dissatisfied with the results of an informal inquiry, she can file a formal complaint with the director or with the director's superior, if there is one. This initiates a formal investigation and may involve lawyers for both sides. The accused perpetrator is at risk for losing his job.

2. If the victim is not satisfied with the outcome of a formal investigation, she can file with the EEOC. Such a filing opens the way for taking the case to court. A victim can bypass several steps and go immediately to the EEOC, but if a camp has a harassment reporting protocol in place, she can hurt her chances in a lawsuit by not following the protocol.

3. She can take the case to court.

As you can see, the camp director has a chance to intervene successfully at the informal inquiry stage to avert formal legal proceedings. Expect that some claims of sexual harassment will not qualify under the legal definition. If you are unsure whether a specific behavior or set of behaviors constitutes sexual harassment, seek legal advice. Once again, though, I recommended that you intervene any time a behavior is viewed as unwelcome and offensive.

Most harassing behaviors can be resolved through simple remedies such as problem-solving, education, and consciousness raising. **Remember, the victim is not seeking a lawsuit. She simply wants the harassing behaviors to end.** An intervention can be anything that stops the perceived harassment. Keep in mind that only in the past half-century have males and females shared the workplace. We are still attempting to learn each other's boundaries, a task that males seem to find especially challenging. Sadly, society offers few positive role models of males respecting female boundaries, and males have little idea of the power of sexual fantasies to warp their perspective on reality.

As a clinician, I have been dismayed at the lengths to which males go to engage a female. A male who asks a female co-worker for a date and is refused is just as likely to continue his efforts as he is to accept her negative response. Such continued efforts constitute sexual harassment. Recall that many males believe that saying "no" to a sexual or romantic overture is simply a female's way of upholding her reputation and not appearing "easy." Thus the male may continue his unwelcome attentions, certain in his fantasy that she will eventually accept.

Harassment Training

The same educational, problem-solving, and consciousness-raising techniques that a director might use to solve other interpersonal problems at camp can be used to intervene in sexual harassment. However, harassment training offers a powerful preemptive strike to keep at least some sexual harassment from ever occurring.

Harassment training is now expected in most industries, and why not in camps as well? A harassment training session during staff week can help clarify many issues. It could present common examples of harassment in camps, protocols for investigating and intervening, and characteristics of human sexuality that lead to harassment, all topics that we have covered in this chapter.

A Proactive Approach

The book *Sex, Power, and Boundaries* (Rutter, 1996) offers valuable advice to males and females that could be included in a training to minimize the occurrence of sexual harassment.

Advice for Men

- Men should be aware of the power of fantasy in their lives and openly acknowledge to themselves that such fantasies are truly unreliable indicators of reality.

- Men should keep their sexual fantasies private unless they are absolutely certain they are welcomed by the other party.

- Men would benefit by learning to live with their fantasies for an extended period of time without seeking physical resolution.

Advice for Women

- Women should recognize any ambiguous signals they might be inadvertently giving off that may invite sexual behavior from males.

- Women should recognize that males may transform trivial occurrences into bases for sexual fantasies.

- Women should learn ways to clearly indicate that specific behaviors are unwelcome when they occur.

- Women could assist males in learning appropriate boundaries by not attempting to criminalize mistakes in their learning process.

Sexual Harassment Policy

The most common intervention for sexual harassment is to create and distribute a sexual harassment policy. This preventive approach warns potential perpetrators of consequences and alerts potential victims to steps they can take if problems arise. A policy can clearly prohibit attempts to retaliate against an accuser and can make managers and supervisors aware of steps they must take if sexual harassment is made known to them.

A written policy that informs perpetrators, victims, and management of the steps to be followed in a sexual harassment case is essential. Too often, supervisors try to handle such complaints on their own rather than informing the administration. Lacking knowledge of the required action steps, a person trying to be helpful could cause an employee to file a formal complaint, thus bypassing an informal investigation that could have ended the harassment.

We provide a sample sexual harassment policy in Chapter 8 as part of an overall plan for camp safety. Wagner (1992) also lays out some elements to consider as you develop your own policy. A good policy has these characteristics:

- **Contained in a separate policy document.** Burying a policy in a staff handbook reduces the chances that it will be read and signals that it is of little importance. A separate policy document shows that the administration takes the subject seriously.

- **Provides clear definition of sexual harassment.** Employees must understand what the law considers sexual harassment along with specific examples that could occur in a camp.

- **Provides a clear, specific resolution protocol.** The protocol can include the step-by-step remedies discussed earlier, ranging from notifying offenders that their behavior is offensive, all the way up to formal legal action.

- **Directs an employee to a neutral party.** Some consultants caution against advising an employee to speak to his or her immediate supervisor because this person is most likely to be the source of the harassment. Each camp should recognize a specific person as the harassment ombudsman.

- **States consequences.** Consequences entail appropriate levels of discipline, including termination.

- **Does not guarantee confidentiality.** If a claim of sexual harassment leads to an investigation, other people will have to become involved. The policy can state that the administration will keep the investigation as confidential as possible and will try to limit the number of people involved.

- **Pledges no retaliation.** An employee who brings a harassment claim to management can experience no retaliation for the action. In addition, a claim of harassment that turns out to be mistaken will result in no penalty for the accuser.

I recommend that you include in your policy document some language to cover more than just sexual harassment. After all, not all harassment qualifies as sexual harassment. What if a male staff member feels that his male boss is treating him disrespectfully? What if one female feels threatened by another female? How does a camp handle relationship violence between co-workers?

Issues such as these do not fall under a sexual harassment policy written specifically for unwanted sexual behaviors and sexual discrimination. In the three examples cited, the behaviors are certainly harassing but are not classified as unlawful sexual harassment. Recall the legal definition of harassment: verbal or physical conduct that belittles or shows hostility or aversion toward an individual based on race, skin color, national origin, age, religion, or disability. If the sole African-American counselor in camp finds himself the victim of a series of unpleasant pranks, he could be experiencing unlawful harassment, though this would not be considered sexual harassment. A more general harassment policy can cover camp employees for a broader range of harassing behaviors and better ensure their emotional well-being in the workplace.

Children participate in a wide range of sexual behaviors, and not all are cause for concern.

6

Childhood Sexuality

For several summers I held the position of program director at a boys' residential camp. One morning, I was awakened by the raised voice of a counselor. He had gotten up early so that he could take a private shower without the presence of other staff. Upon entering the shower facility, he confronted two ten-year-old campers completely naked and fondling each other's penises. Totally unprepared for what he saw, this counselor hurled out a stream of curses, demanded that the boys get dressed, and marched them to my office. Imagine my surprise to be startled awake by an angry and confused counselor claiming that he had two "gay boys" on his hands, with the two children themselves on the verge of tears.

How would you handle such an incident? I have asked the same question at numerous workshops and conferences and gotten very different answers. Some directors would have sent the two boys home. Others would have written up the male staff member for his reaction to the situation. Some would have called up parents and asked their opinion. Others would have done nothing. These responses mirror the ongoing battle between restrictive and permissive approaches to sexuality discussed in Chapter 1. Indeed, childhood sexuality is one of the major arenas for such conflict.

In this chapter we examine child sexual behavior under the age of twelve. Childhood sexuality may differ in tone and content from teenage and adult sexuality, but it is still sexuality. In the United States, we seem to have an especially hard time recognizing children as sexual beings, which leaves both us and the children ill-prepared to cope with natural expressions of sexuality.

[In the United States] we attempt to protect children from even knowing there is such a thing as sexuality. This protection, as traditionally carried out, has meant that the child is shielded from all adult and adolescent, and many childhood, sexual experiences. There is no modeling on the part of the adolescents or adults, sex talk in the presence of children is avoided, nonlabeling or mislabeling of sexual parts and activities occurs, no sexual experimentation with peers or siblings is allowed, and no age-appropriate sex education for younger children is sanctioned. North American children know the least about sexuality, received their sexual knowledge at older ages, and are least prepared for adult sexual experience…(Martinson, 1997, pp. 36–37).*

Freud theorized that young children undergo a period of "latency," or disinterest in sexuality. Psychologists refuted this idea years ago, although some people still cling to the latency concept. I assure you that many of your young campers are engaging in sexual behaviors. Some of them will have sexual behavior problems that need immediate intervention and possibly even termination from the camp community. The good news is that not all expressions of child sexuality are bad or even worrisome, and most require a camp director to do very little.

A Process of Exploration

Scientists have been hard at work to help us understand and accept the nature of child sexuality. Having refuted the idea of latency, they are trying to catalog the sexual behaviors expected between infancy and puberty. Scientists use the term *normative* to describe these expected behaviors because they represent the norm for specific age ranges.

Researchers use various methods in their work on normative sexual behaviors of children. Some interview parents, caregivers, or teachers. Others record their observations of children at play. Still others ask adults to recall their own sexual experiences as children. These research methods are subject to error but, on the whole, one finding stands out: **Children participate in a wide range of sexual behaviors**.

Expressions of sexuality evolve as a child matures. We do not expect an infant to exhibit the same sexual behaviors as a six-year-old, nor do we expect the sexual behaviors of a six-year-old to resemble those of a teenager. But there is no clear line showing when this or that behavior starts or stops at a particular age. The evolution of sexual behaviors is an ongoing process of development.

Young children and infants (ages four and below) typically exhibit sexual behaviors that focus on themselves. They have minimal inhibitions regarding such behaviors. For example, a child rubbing his or her genitals is not uncommon. Young children may demonstrate an interest in the bodies of others, including those of other children and adults.

As the child matures and begins to have more peer involvement, it is expected that a greater variety of sexual exploration will occur. However, this increase is accompanied by more inhibition. Most children have been socialized by the age of four that certain contact with one's own body or the body of another is "wrong." Parents and caregivers may not see as much playful sexual interaction and sexual inquisitiveness as demonstrated in the earlier years, but the drive to explore is by no means gone. Much of the behavior has simply gone "underground," away from the eyes of older individuals. In addition, some children incorporate the restrictions of their caretakers into themselves

---

*From F. M. Martinson, "Sexual development in infancy and childhood." In G. Ryan & S. Lane (Eds.), *Juvenile Sexual Offending.* Copyright ©1997 by Jossey-Bass Publishers. Reprinted by permission of John Wiley & Sons, Inc.

and thus avoid sexual contact with themselves or others. This in no way means that sexual interest and curiosity have abated.

To summarize, sexual development is an exploratory process. As the child matures from infancy to very early puberty, we should expect:

- Increased variety in sexual behaviors.

- Increasing use of peers as objects of exploration.

- Less likelihood that parents and caregivers will actually see such behaviors.

We mentioned earlier the special difficulty we have in accepting expressions of childhood sexuality. It is noteworthy that among the research finding is that most sexual behaviors occurring in children—even those we consider shocking, such as sexual contact between young brothers and sisters—are not really considered remarkable in other parts of the world.

Normative Sexual Behaviors

Scientists have cataloged a variety of sexual behaviors that are possible and expected during childhood. Not all children exhibit every behavior. We cite the age when specific behaviors are expected to occur, but these are just general guidelines, as children develop physically and cognitively at different rates. It is simply impossible to pinpoint the ages when sexual behaviors occur, and even clinicians shy away from using rigid timelines.

Although none of these normative behaviors indicates a sexual problem, neither does their presence indicate that no sexual problem or underlying pathology exists. Later we will explore when these behaviors should be further investigated and not simply labeled acceptable for the child's age. For now, though, consider the following behaviors not necessarily problematic but expected and anticipated by those who care for children.

Touching Oneself / Masturbation

Touching one's genitals is the most common sexual behavior in children. Young children between infancy and sixteen months of age typically demonstrate a random pattern of self-stimulation, often referred to as "genital play." In males, true masturbation—massaging the penis or rubbing it against an object—begins at approximately fifteen months. In females, the onset of masturbation is about the same, but the behavior is more irregular. At about age three, females begin to place a blanket or toy between the legs in the area of the genitals. Through these early self-explorations, children learn to associate touching oneself with pleasure, and as they grow older they become more consistent in the behavior. At the same time, they learn that society frowns upon open displays of such behavior, and they know not to touch themselves in public. Touching oneself and masturbation continue throughout the lifespan but are more prevalent in males. Self-stimulation occurs but is hidden from the view of parents and caregivers.

Example: Cabin counselor Wayne wakes early for his morning run. The previous night was the hottest of the season thus far, and sleeping under a sheet was unbearable.

Better to risk mosquito bites than a sleepless night due to the humidity. As he scrutinizes the six nine-year-old boys in his cabin, he cannot help but laugh quietly. None of them have sheets covering them, and four of them, though soundly sleeping, have at least one hand down their pants and are obviously grasping their penises.

Observing Others' Bodies

Young children below the age of four may not have been socialized yet to understand the concept of privacy. They may enter the bathroom when another person occupies it. They may stare intently at another person as he or she takes a shower. This is due not to sexual interest as an adult might experience but rather to curiosity about the human body. Older children may still watch but are more furtive in their observations. In addition, they show an increasing interest in the bodies of peers.

Example: At the daily administration meeting after breakfast, the male and female program directors share similar problems with the camp director. A cabin of eight-year-old boys and a cabin of ten-year-old girls are experiencing internal stress. Children from both cabins are reporting that a cabin mate is "gay" because he or she looks at them while they undress.

Showing Genitals

The exposure of genitals is common in childhood and is typically innocuous behavior. Young children are quite comfortable walking around with little or no clothing. They show no more concern about exposing their genitals than they do about exposing their hands. They soon learn, though, that certain parts of their bodies are private. It may be okay to expose arms and legs during the summer, but adults do not walk around with their genitals exposed. Even if the idea of privacy is never taught directly, children easily imitate what they see occurring around them. The overall message is that the genital areas are private, different from other parts of the body. As they are socialized away from exposing their genitals, such behavior becomes less common, especially in front of adults, but curiosity drives children to continue comparing their bodies to others.

Example: A camp director receives an angry phone call from a parent. Her child reported that, as the boys in his cabin changed for their swim, they would have contests to see who had the longest penis. They did this quietly so as not to alert the staff member outside.

Asking Sexual Questions / Talking About Sex

Gathering information about one's own body and that of others is expected behavior during childhood. With direct observation either not available or off limits, asking questions is a reasonable way to try to acquire such information. Children under age four are usually quite naïve—but often direct—in their questions about the body and sexuality. The asking of personal sexual questions of staff is one of the most common and uncomfortable sexual issues for cabin counselors. Children learn early on that asking sexual questions of adults makes them uncomfortable, silent, and sometimes even angry. Socialized to not discuss sexual matters, older children turn away from adults and rely more and more on their peers and the media for sexual information.

In addition to freely asking questions, children feel free to talk about sex. Parents have described to me their mortification from such incidents. One mother had taught her son to name all his body parts, including his penis and testicles. At a party for one of his friends, this four-year-old proceeded to announce to the parents in attendance that he had "a penis and nobody is allowed to touch it." While the other parents laughed, the boy's mother cringed in embarrassment. Such innocent statements are to be expected for younger children.

Even below the age of four, sexual jokes occur. As children mature into older childhood, such jokes become more graphic. Adults who reprimand their children do not stop such behavior but only ensure that it occurs when an adult cannot hear it. Camp staff (including myself) have overheard young campers talking about sex, sometimes graphically, and sometimes in a joking manner.

Example: Cassandra is on duty for her unit that night. As she makes her rounds about the cabins, she hears several eleven-year-old girls laughing quietly in an attempt not to attract attention to themselves. She shakes her head in bewilderment as she listens to their conversation. They are discussing possible romantic liaisons among the staff. One girl asks the others if they think that Cassandra is a "virgin." They go onto debate the merits of sexual contact in camp.

Normative Behaviors That May Cause Concern

Touching oneself, exposing oneself, observing the bodies of others, and talking about sex are fairly well accepted as appropriate behaviors for children under age twelve. Though caregivers may not condone such behaviors, the behaviors are not especially controversial. The remainder of the list of childhood sexual behaviors is more apt to cause concern for adults. Because children have become socialized to hide sexual behavior, these behaviors may seem quite controversial when we do encounter them.

As with the previous list, the following behaviors do not indicate a sexual behavior problem. Adults may be much more uncomfortable with the behaviors, but this does not warrant panic. Few sexual behaviors in themselves automatically indicate a sexual behavior problem. A host of other factors must be considered before making such an assumption.

Dating

Children in the middle childhood years may mimic the adults they see in real life and in the media by having a "girlfriend" or "boyfriend." Due to the same-sex segregation that occurs in childhood play groups, such "relationships" are often nothing more than words. Children have little interest in spending time with their supposed "date." Older children begin to experiment with dating, but initial dates are usually mutually uncomfortable rehearsals for the dating behaviors of adolescence and adulthood. Even children who report "going steady" actually spend little time with each other. Due to individual differences in children's physical and cognitive development, some children will take dating very seriously even as their same-aged peers have little interest in such matters.

Example: During the camp carnival, a group of eight-year-old males asks their counselor to "set them up" with girls from the youngest female unit. This he does. Within a half-hour, the campers report—most with relief—that their "girlfriends" have dumped them.

Touching Others

Children below age four touch each other quite innocently in their exploration of everything that surrounds them. Males and females touch each other and explore each other's bodies quite freely. However, when "caught," or when witnessing a friend who has been discovered in the activity, they quickly realize that such behavior is especially likely to anger adults. It therefore becomes hidden.

Older children begin to practice the sexual behaviors that they will take up in earnest at puberty. Besides kissing, hugging, and holding hands, children older than eight may fondle each other's genitals and even rub their bodies against each other while clothed, in an imitation of sexual intercourse. These various forms of physical contact can occur between children of the same sex or the opposite sex. The children discover that sexual contact can be physically pleasurable.

Example: At a "buddy check" during swim period, a unit leader realizes that two of his ten-year-old campers are missing. As the lifeguard initiates the missing bather procedure, he sends one counselor to their unit to check if the campers are there. Upon entering the cabin, the counselor finds the two boys lying on a bed, fully dressed but one on top of the other and engaged in intense kissing.

Penetration

Infants and young children may attempt to insert their fingers or other objects into their rectum or vagina. They stop if pain occurs. Children above the age of eight, but usually around eleven or twelve, may actually attempt intercourse. This sexual behavior is thought to be the least common of the ones we have examined. Though a male may not be able to create sperm at a young age, he can still achieve an erection and use it to penetrate the vagina or rectum. This exploration is preparation for the more sophisticated sexual behaviors that will occur after puberty and are an immediate source of physical pleasure. Because puberty can occur earlier for some individuals than others, older children may well be able to have sex with ejaculation.

Example: A camp director reports her mixed emotions over discontinuing the customary free time she gives to campers for one hour after the evening meal. The previous week, two eleven-year-old campers were found having intercourse in a cabin during this time. Though both campers said they consented to the behavior, the fear of repercussions from parents was enough that the director felt justified in completely stopping this period of free time.

Behaviors Indicating a Problem

Not all childhood expressions of sexuality are harmless. Some acts may signal a true underlying problem needing medical, psychological, and possibly legal intervention as well as immediate removal from the camp premises. Our aim is to help you differentiate such problematic behavior from more normative expressions of sexuality.

Most camp administrators would have no problem classifying a ten-year-old boy who throws a female peer to the ground and fondles her as an immediate risk to camp safety, but not all situations are so obvious. The general ambivalence and lack of knowledge regarding childhood sexuality in the United States influence a director's judgment. Directors with a more permissive slant toward childhood sexuality may be willing to classify an act as a normative display, while directors with a more restrictive slant may be quick to determine that the act is inappropriate. Any less-than-clear-cut situation is interpreted through our own cultural mindset but, as we learned in Chapter 1, reliance on our own perspective is not necessarily the most accurate method to judge the appropriateness of an act.

The impact of personal perspective is seen when the camp director has to formulate policy with regard to sexual behavior. A director may decide that any display—by either staff or campers—is sufficient reason to sever the "perpetrator's" relationship with the camp. Such a policy is certain to "throw the baby out with the bath water." Children displaying normative sexual behaviors will be sent home just as surely as those who display flagrant problem behaviors.

Camps host a wide array of children each season. Some children will show little interest in sexual pursuits. Some will exhibit sexual behaviors that are clearly normative. Some will behave in semi-sexual ways that make staff and possibly other campers uncomfortable—for example, appearing to know too much about sex for their age—yet will never actually do anything that can be labeled as harmful. Some will perform dangerous or threatening sexual acts that are clearly not normative. Camp administration fervently hopes for campers who show little interest in sexual pursuits, but they must prepare to deal with a full range of normative and non-normative expressions of sexuality.

An Epidemic of Child Offenders?

Over the past decade, the news media have given much attention to violence among youth. A research report on local coverage by television stations throughout California found that 55 percent of news stories about youth concerned violence committed by or against them (Dorfman 1997). This is not just a California phenomenon but extends to the entire nation. A similar study of the nation's leading newspapers found that 40 percent of reports on children concerned crime and violence (Kunkel, 1994).

One type of story that never fails to attract media attention is when a child is the perpetrator of a crime. Cases of children who have committed heinous crimes—including murder—make good press. Examinations of the news coverage on childhood offenders find two recurring elements: depictions of young criminals and their crimes, and "evidence" that the number of such young offenders is on the rise.

What is the reality? Is the number of violent and predatory children growing? If this were true, camp directors would indeed have something to worry about. Some of these highly dangerous children could be campers in an upcoming season. Fortunately, there is little evidence to justify this fear. As reported in an Office of Juvenile Justice and Delinquency Programming Bulletin geared for juvenile justice professionals:

> [J]ustice professionals tend to accumulate memories of exceptional cases. Every twelve-year-old killer is remembered, even though such cases are few in number. After many years of working with juveniles, justice professionals may believe that the problem of young killers is getting worse because of the numbers that have been encountered during their careers.

> [T]he news media have increased their reporting of crime, especially violent crimes by the very young. Today, the public hears about every incident, whether it happened in a different town or on a different continent. Moreover, the details of every incident are repeated several times—at arrest, trial, sentencing, etc. The growing publicity about these cases may suggest to the public that they are occurring more frequently, even if juvenile justice trends indicate otherwise (Butts, 1997, p. 8).

Juvenile justice professionals are not the only ones accumulating memories of exceptional cases. Camp directors, staff, parents, and even campers can likely recall such incidents. The statistical reality, though, is that today's serious and violent juvenile offenders are not significantly younger than those of ten or fifteen years ago. The actual number of offenders aged fourteen or younger remains relatively small in comparison to the number of older juvenile offenders seen in the legal system. All in all, there is no epidemic of children committing serious crimes, and those incidents that involve a violent child are actually quite rare. Our awareness of such incidents seems to have increased, but the actual incidents have not.

Children Who Commit Sexual Offenses

Although rare, there are youth who commit serious sexual crimes. Researchers have found cases of children under the age of twelve who have committed rape and molestation. More have been found to commit non-contact offenses such as exposing themselves and masturbating in public.

Children who commit inappropriate sexual acts are a fairly new research population. Though researchers have worked with adult sexual offenders for the last several decades, their work with teenage sexual offenders is only about a decade old. Only in the past several years have researchers even recognized that some children commit the same crimes as adult sexual offenders. Thus the research with this population is far from comprehensive. Many researchers have fought political and social battles even to get these young offenders recognized.

We can assume that camps will reflect the same statistics as the rest of the nation. That is, the majority of children entering camps will exhibit only normative sexual behaviors, a slight minority will be sexually inappropriate but not necessarily dangerous, a very few will display aggressive sexual behaviors, and, overall, non-contact offenses will far outnumber violent sexual behaviors.

In the remainder of this chapter, we take a closer look at certain problem sexual behaviors. Although they can appear in the same child, for convenience we divide them into two categories:

- Sexually intrusive behaviors that are not necessarily criminal but that make others uncomfortable, such as standing too close or seeking unusual amounts of physical contact such as hugs and kisses.

- Clinical sexual behavior problems include the use of aggression and/or violence.

Sexually Intrusive Behaviors

Sexually intrusive behaviors reflect a poor understanding of personal boundaries. Children who violate personal boundaries cause discomfort to adults and possibly even to their peers. We expect more intrusive behaviors from children since they have had less time for socialization, but such behaviors can and do occur across the lifespan. People who interact with such intrusive persons typically feel confused or invaded.

Following are some of the sexually intrusive behaviors that children lacking a sense of personal boundaries may demonstrate:

- Walking around nude.

- Walking in a sexual way.

- Talking in a sexual way.

- Revealing too much knowledge about sexual matters.

- Non-aggressive rubbing or touching of other people's bodies.

- Kissing and hugging of strangers.

- Excessive requests for physical contact.

- Looking through another person's personal items.

- Drawing pictures of a sexual nature.

- Staring at the body parts of another person.

True stories of sexually intrusive camp behaviors easily come to mind:

- A male counselor was confused when an eight-year-old female camper wanted to sit on his lap during a campfire.

- A female staff member was dumbfounded when a child returned from the shower room without clothing. The girl had walked through the entire camp property undressed.

- A male counselor found that his underwear had been stolen. Immediately assuming that this was the result of a camp prank, he later found that one of his campers had "borrowed" them to see what they felt like.

- An arts-and-crafts instructor was alarmed to find that the picture a camper was using crayons to draw consisted of a couple engaged in intercourse.

Camp directors repeatedly express concern over campers who seem to have far too much knowledge about sex. This is likely to come to the director's attention when another camper complains or a staff member overhears an exchange. Other campers wear provocative clothing. Many directors have reported on the increasing use of sexualized movements in dance routines in talent shows. As these examples indicate, the problem is widespread. However, though such children may cause others to feel discomfort, they do not necessarily need a psychological intervention or termination from the camp. A review of the list of intrusive behaviors shows that some of them could even be classified as variations of normative sexuality.

When a child displays sexually inappropriate behavior, many adults jump to the conclusion that he or she must have experienced sexual abuse. This could be true, but another factor could also explain the behavior: the lack of clear boundaries in the household. Before deciding whether a specific behavior is a normative display or truly indicates an underlying disorder, it is important to look at the family background of these youth.

When I started out as a parent educator, I was stunned by some of the parental boundary issues I encountered. For example, one mother lived in a one-room apartment. When her boyfriend came over, there was no other place to have sex. Though the couple waited until the child was supposedly asleep, the child's behavior in the schoolyard indicated that she had witnessed far more than her mother could believe. The child would ask peers to lie on top of her and grind against her while she made moaning noises. The school administration initially thought she had been sexually abused, but an investigation revealed no such evidence. The child was merely acting out what she had seen in the home.

Poor boundaries in the household can be the major source of intrusive sexual behaviors in children. Even youth who display more severe sexual behaviors have likely experienced such a household environment. It is easy to see why a child raised in an environment that lacked clear boundaries would have trouble with boundaries in a camp setting. For example, a child raised in a home that does not recognize the bathroom as a "private" space, that allows other family members to enter even when it is already occupied, would not hesitate to enter a bathroom occupied by a counselor. While non-family members might find such behavior disturbing, for the child it is only natural.

These are some of the boundary violations in a household that could result in confusing behavior by a camper:

- Children watch adult material, including outright pornography, on television, cable, video, DVD, and the Internet. Parents may not be aware that the child is occupied with such material or may even approve of such behavior. Parents may also leave adult materials within easy reach of children.

- Children observe sexual behavior in their immediate home environment. As we have seen, the family may live in a one-bedroom apartment that allows no other space for adult sexual activity. Some parents may ingest substances that lower their inhibitions, resulting in sexual activity performed directly in front of children. Some parents may confide in a child to meet their own emotional needs, informing the child of very personal aspects of their adult lives, including sexual activity. Parents themselves may have been raised in homes that lacked boundaries and are repeating the pattern with their own children.

- Children have been raised in environments in which their bodily boundaries are not respected. This can include sexual abuse but also less obvious means such as bathing a child well past an appropriate age, subjecting the child to massages or other touching that is uncomfortable, or coercing the child to touch or massage another person.

- Children have been raised in homes where privacy is not respected. There may be no locks on bathroom or bedroom doors, and other family members may enter without knocking or requesting permission.

In all of these examples, the child is a witness to or a forced participant in an activity that is inappropriate for his or her age or is not granted personal space in which to experience privacy. The child has heard, seen, or been forced to perform an activity that interfered with his or her understanding of appropriate boundaries. Although the inappropriate behaviors may be tolerated if not approved in the immediate household, the child is certain to encounter problems outside the home.

Sexually Aggressive and Compulsive Behaviors

When a child demonstrates aggressive sexual behavior toward him- or herself or in interactions with others, is unable to stop the problem behaviors, or elicits complaints from other campers, a camp director must acknowledge that he or she faces a serious sexual behavior problem. Even if the director is an expert in child welfare and has the most professional, most mature staff working in the camp, these youth have problems that cannot readily be solved, especially in a camp setting. Some may require only a few therapeutic sessions to learn to manage the problem; others may take years of intensive individual, group, and family treatment. Camp directors are best advised to allow other professionals to intervene with these youth.

We have said that normative childhood sexuality is a process of exploration. That process has certain characteristics:

- Participants in exploratory acts find them mutually enjoyable.

- Children do not experience the sexual sensations that teenagers and adults do. Rather, they find the encounter playful.

- No threats, coercion, or bribery are involved.

- None of the participants experience anger or resentment, as both willingly participate in the act and are able to stop at any time.

- Children who are asked by adults to stop this activity will either stop or be certain that they are not "caught in the act" in future encounters.

In contrast, we may encounter children who are aggressive and/or compulsive in their sexuality. Their process has very different characteristics:

- The children often use some type of force to elicit participation in sexual acts from others.

- They find no joy or playfulness in sexual acts.

- Those subjected to the sexual acts are uncooperative, unwilling participants.

- The behavior leaves someone emotionally or physically hurt, whether the victim or the perpetrator.

Van Dam (2001) explains these contrasting scenarios on the basis of differences in power and knowledge:

> [T]wo children with equal power and knowledge touching each other's genitalia without knowing to maintain secrecy are engaging in normal sex play, and their behavior can be safely ignored. Sexual activity between two children would qualify as sexual abuse, however, if power and coercion were used. If one child is bigger, more aggressive, older, has advanced knowledge, or in any way threatens the other child, then the situation is one of abuse (p. 50).

Children who exhibit compulsiveness in their sexual behaviors, and are therefore unable to control themselves, often experience pain in the acts. For example, a group of nine-year-old girls approached an assistant camp director to complain about one of their cabin mates. The girl in question would take a shampoo bottle and insert it into her vagina before falling asleep each night. She would cry while she was doing this due to the pain it would cause. The fact that a sexual activity was causing pain was enough to warrant concern on the part of the camp administration. Insertion of objects into the vagina might be considered normative sexual behavior, but it was clearly not so when it caused pain and especially when it continued despite the obvious disapproval of peers. The assistant director explained to the girl that this was inappropriate behavior and that she needed to stop immediately if she wanted to remain at camp. That night, however, the girl initiated the behavior once again. The assistant director had no choice but to act on the promised dismissal. She later learned that this child came from an environment of abuse and neglect.

Aggressive and compulsive sexual behavior problems usually begin in the family environment. In comparison to the sexually intrusive youth, compulsive and aggressive youth have far more tumultuous backgrounds. Whereas intrusive youth may have witnessed or experienced sexual acts that were far above their levels of comprehension, compulsive and aggressive youth may have been subjected to repeated acts of sexual and physical abuse as well as neglect. Though the research into this population is sparse, the damaging backgrounds of these youth are widely accepted as a causal factor. Researchers agree that children with severe sexual behavior problems are raised in families that have high rates of physical violence, neglect, and sexual abuse. A child raised in such a dysfunctional family will not necessarily act out in camp but is much more likely to act out than a child not raised in such an environment.

Youth who exhibit sexually aggressive and compulsive behaviors are often, but not always, the victims of sexual abuse. These acts occur repeatedly over a long period of time, and the perpetrator—or perpetrators, as there can be more than one—is someone with ongoing access to the victim, often a family member or a close friend of the family. The sexual abuse often involves force and violence. Penetration of the anus and/or vagina is common, but these young victims may also experience a wide variety of sexual abuses. Research suggests that the physical violence is an even bigger factor in sexual behavior problems than the sexual abuse. Researchers are examining how a child learns to associate non-sexual physical violence to sexual acting out. Several theories have been advanced, but with no definitive answer.

A child who experiences ongoing sexual abuse often comes from a family that has numerous other problems. As mentioned earlier, weak boundaries are inherent in these families. They also have high rates of parental separation, domestic violence, substance abuse, and poor parent-child relationships. Most of these families have more than one victim of sexual abuse, whether this is another child or a parent. In short, the families of sexually aggressive and compulsive youth are often highly stressed and dysfunctional. Even if a child does disclose abuse to an unknowing parent, it is unlikely that he or she will be believed.

I want to dispel the myth that children who have been sexually abused are destined to have psychological problems. This is simply not true. A child who is abused only a few times without force or violence, who has not experienced penetration, who comes from a stable family environment, and who has at least one caregiver who responds with a protective stance against further abuse may suffer few, if any, consequences. Even children who come from the highly dysfunctional families characteristic of aggressive and compulsive youth may experience few overt problems. **Camp directors should not assume that a victim of sexual abuse is a danger to other camp participants.**

Studies of adult sexual offenders shed some light on sexually aggressive and compulsive youth. Researchers have found that adult sexual offenders often had numerous victims, sometimes hundreds, before they were finally apprehended. These offenders began their activities when they were still youths themselves—even preadolescents—and committed offenses against others throughout their developmental years. This correlates with the statistic that sexually aggressive children begin to demonstrate problems between the ages of six and nine. Even at these young ages, multiple victims are possible. Research documents that, among youth offenders, the number of victims ranges from one to nine. The victims are likely to be even younger than the offender, ranging in age from four to seven. Few of these victims are strangers. They are either family members or are somehow known to the offending youth.

Although we might assume that sexually compulsive and aggressive behaviors are more prevalent among males than females, the evidence says otherwise. A significant minority of preadolescent perpetrators of sexual abuse are girls, and females demonstrate sexual actions that are just as aggressive as males.

It is almost impossible to recognize children who may be sexual offenders until problematic behaviors occur. Some of these children experience academic problems, non-sexual behavior problems, and hyperactivity. They often have poor social skills and have difficulty making friends. Some are impulsive and easily angered. Others are exceedingly timid and cautious. The fact is, many children who attend camp each summer have similar characteristics but are not sexually aggressive. The rare sexually aggressive or compulsive child appears to be a "challenge" rather than an actual danger to others. The only way to know the difference is a comprehensive and honest transfer of pertinent information between parents and camp staff. The more risk factors in the child's background, the more likely the child will present as a problem in the camp setting.

What to Do?

The following letter appeared in *Camping Magazine*'s "In the Trenches" column.

Dear Bob:

It has come to our attention this fall that we had a problem in our boys' middle camp that we were unaware of.

Evidently there was a widespread "game" which the boys supposedly called "humping" where boys who were eleven, twelve, and thirteen would simulate sexual intercourse using a pillow and, perhaps in one or two cases, each other.

When other boys were involved it was always with clothes on, though in the cabin, the game when "played" with a pillow might occur with just underwear or a bathing suit...(Ditter, 2003, p. 59).

How would you respond to this incident? After reading this chapter, I hope you are not too surprised by the behavior of these youths. You may not like the behavior, but you can recognize that it is age-appropriate sexual exploration.

Contrast this with the concern of a parent writing in a *CampLine* article about an incident that occurred in a day camp:

[N]ot only as a parent, but as a camp director, was I totally shocked when my eight-year-old son Michael told me one night between sobs that another boy at his day camp had been touching his private areas. Michael and I spent the rest of the evening rehearsing what he should do if this were to happen again. I reassured him that he had done nothing wrong. I rubbed his tummy and he practiced saying, "Stop! I'm telling a counselor." Michael insisted that we do this role-play at least ten times before he finally fell asleep (Anonymous, 2003, p. 13).

This parent had every right to be angry, shocked, and concerned for the child's safety. Michael was a victim—he was afraid and did not voluntarily participate in the behavior. He was bullied into compliance. But what of the parents of the children who feigned sexual intercourse with a pillow? They too were presumably angry, shocked, and concerned for their children's welfare. But in their case, there was no clear victim. The parents may have been offended by the children's sexual behavior, but did the children really do anything wrong?

Camp directors face a challenge that will not soon disappear—how to respond to normative sexual behavior between children of the same age and developmental level. A camp director who encounters aggressive sexual behavior, whether self-inflicted or acted out upon others, is obligated to intervene. But the response to normative sexual behavior is far more complicated.

As a camp director, you must prepare to be caught up in the societal fray over childhood sexuality. If you tolerate normative sexual behavior, you risk parental anger and mistrust. A director who tries to explain to a concerned parent that normative sexual behavior is not unexpected among children may be greeted with hostility. Though the director has research on his or her side, the emotional state of the parent may prevent meaningful dialogue. Thus if you believe in and accept the data on normative childhood sexuality, you may be considered "soft" on childhood sexuality and tolerant of sexual abuse when, in fact, you are actually more knowledgeable than the concerned parent. On the other hand, if you are intolerant of childhood sexuality, you risk inflicting unnecessary embarrassment or actual psychological harm by treating normative displays as major acts of wrongdoing.

A way to frame your own camp's response is to consider that adults have specific responsibilities in regard to children's sexual development. Adults must:

- Protect children from sexually inappropriate behavior on the part of adults and peers.

- Teach children about sex and its many complexities.

- Socialize children to perform sexually appropriate behaviors.

- Model appropriate sexual behaviors.

All camps share in at least three of these responsibilities with parents. Camps can aim to protect their campers and staff from inappropriate sexual behaviors. Camps can socialize children as to appropriate and inappropriate sexual behaviors in the camp setting. Camps can hire and train staff that demonstrate appropriate social interactions between males and females. When it comes to teaching children about sex, though, camps differ in their practices. Some camps ask parents to discuss sex with their children prior to camp attendance, sometimes even including a sheet of pertinent sexual information. Most camps refrain from this and leave sex education exclusively to the parents.

When expressions of childhood sexuality occur, a camp director must formulate a response based on the mission and philosophy of the camp, his or her personal beliefs, and the details of the presenting incident.

Response to Discovered Sexual Activity

When staff come across an episode of sexual activity between campers, the result is often spontaneous and negative—the campers are shamed for activity that may very well be normative for their ages. Shame is certainly not an experience camp professionals want associated with the field.

Following is a process that camps might want to consider when sexual incidents occur between campers. The process depends upon camp administration having already formulated its philosophy on camper sexual activity and shared this with staff. Staff are often in a state of agitation immediately after stumbling across sexual activity. Lacking knowledge of camp policy, they may respond in ways that are unwelcome in the camp environment, could have lasting detrimental effects on the campers, and put the camp legally at risk.

When a staff member discovers camper sexual activity, the following steps can be taken to formulate a proper response.

1. Calmly tell the campers to stop the activity immediately.

The message must be delivered in a non-shaming, non-threatening, non-judgmental way. This sounds easy on paper, but in real life it can be challenging. A staff member may be tempted to scream, curse, or lay hands on the campers, but the more effective course is to calmly and firmly tell them to stop. The aim is not to establish that the sexual activity is wrong, only that *it is not acceptable at camp*.

Use phrases like:

"I need you to stop this right now. This camp doesn't allow this activity."

"It's time to go outside with the rest of the group. Are you both okay?"

"It's okay to be curious about each other. It would be better, though, to ask the camp nurse about any questions."

"Romantic and sexual feelings are normal. We just don't act on them at camp."

Avoid phrases like:

"That's disgusting!"

"What the hell is wrong with you?"

"Wait till I tell everybody what you do!"

"You faggot/dyke."

"Your parents are going to kill you."

2. Report the activity to camp administration.

No staff member should rely solely on personal judgment when sexual incidents occur. All occurrences must be reported to the director.

3. Determine whether coercion was involved.

This is the director's responsibility. By talking to the campers involved, the director attempts to learn whether coercion was used. This is a clue to whether the sexual activity was normative or indicates a more serious problem. Again, the tone of the conversation should not be judgmental or punitive. The interview should answer these questions:

- Were threats used?

- Could both campers have stopped the activity if they wanted to?

- Were bribes used to engage one child in the act?

- Did one child have authority or power over another?

- Is there an age difference of more than three years between the campers?

- Was one child noticeably bigger or stronger than the other?

- Did both campers have an understanding about the activity before it occurred?

- Did both campers agree to the activity before it occurred?

- Is one camper developmentally slower than the other?

4. Base a proper response on the details of the case.

The director selects one or more responses appropriate to the seriousness of the offense. The range of responses can include:

- Remind the campers that sexual behavior is not acceptable in camp.

- Contact parents of both campers even if no coercion occurred.

- Send the coercive child home.

- Call the police in to handle a serious case.

- Contact the agency that maintains your state's registry for incidents of child abuse to learn the specific details that apply to your camp. Acts that involve coercion, force, aggression, and/or an age difference between perpetrator and victim may need to be reported to this agency, which usually performs its own evaluation.

Response to Sexually Intrusive Behavior

Staff who observe or experience sexually intrusive behavior can use the same approach as with any discovered sexual activity: Calmly tell the camper to stop the behavior, and report the behavior to the director. However, the director's response calls for a slightly different set of interview questions. Simple questions are used to explore the child's understanding of the behavior:

"Why did you ask to sit on the counselor's lap during the talent show?"

"Why did you walk to the shower house with no clothes on?"

On occasion, the answer will indicate sexual abuse of some type, and the camp must follow through using the protocol in place for such occurrences. More often, though, the answer will indicate poor household boundaries. In such cases, the camp director can intervene directly with these steps:

---

1. Explain to the child that the behavior is not appropriate for camp.

2. Ask the child if he or she can control the behavior.

3. Tell the child that if it happens again, he or she will be sent home from camp.

4. Contact the parents if this seems warranted.

If this direct intervention does not succeed, it may be time to send the child home. The following signs indicate that a child's behavior needs further investigation and intervention above what a camp is capable of completing.

- The child appears unable to stop the behavior.

- The behavior continues in spite of a request to stop.

- The behavior increases in frequency or intensity.

- Other children complain about the behavior.

Most sexually intrusive behaviors lack aggressive intent. The child is not attempting to hurt another person; he or she has simply never learned proper boundaries. You may be surprised at how successful a request to stop the behavior can be. If the child cannot stop the behavior, or becomes aggressive in performing it, we have moved into the realm of true sexual behavior problems that require removal from the camp to ensure the safety of other campers.

A Note on Teenage Sex

This chapter has focused on the sexual behaviors of children under the age of twelve. This has left out a sizable chunk of the camp population: teenagers. Teenage sexuality continues the exploration of childhood sexual development but increasingly within the confines of dating relationships. Such relationships experience the same problems that were addressed in earlier chapters, including differences between male and female sexuality, lack of dialogue about sex, and misinterpretation of cues.

What is the quality of adolescent sexual relationships? Researchers have spent much more time on the quantifying aspects of sexual activity than on the quality aspects. Judith Levine courageously addressed this in her book, *Harmful to Minors* (2002), and found research on the quality of adolescent sexual experience to be virtually nonexistent. "Imagine," she comments, "what it would be to apply to the National Institutes of Health to find out about sixteen-year-olds' fantasies, their desires, their arousal or orgasm? That, in the eyes of many influential Congress members, would border on sexual abuse" (p. 134).

Levine believes, and my clinical work with adolescents confirms, that much of adolescent sexual activity is less than fulfilling. Even for adults, achieving sexual pleasure takes practice. Surveys of adolescent females often find regret to be the main emotion associated with early sexual experiences. But lack of pleasure with sex should not be taken as evidence that sexual activity is wrong or inappropriate for adolescents. Maybe, as some propose, adolescents need education on obtaining pleasure from sexual acts as much as they need information on preventing pregnancy and disease.

The average age of onset of puberty has markedly decreased. Children show signs of puberty as early as eight years old, which would have been quite uncommon in the not-too-distant past. What camp director has not encountered a new camper who *must* be in their mid-teens, only to find that the camper is twelve or younger? Because adolescents achieve reproductive capability and experience sexual interest at increasingly younger ages, an emerging issue for adolescents is that social development often lags behind physical and biological development. Adolescents do not attain cognitive maturity until between the ages of fourteen and sixteen.

Teenagers who start dating early face greater interpersonal challenges than those who start later, for several reasons.

- Younger teens often have not developed their perspective-taking ability—the ability to perceive an issue through "someone else's eyes"—and can be quite self-centered. This cognitive immaturity has an influence on social maturity.

- They have had less time to learn and practice the necessary social skills for a romantic relationship. Thus they are more likely to rely on the social skills learned in same-sex relationships.

- They may be unprepared to cope with sexual sensations, emotions, and thoughts. These are a source of great excitement for adolescents but also a source of great confusion. Ill-equipped to manage their urges, young teens may fall into harassing behaviors or sexual assault.

The young teenage males that I work with who have been arrested for sexual offenses are mostly not "bad" kids. They simply cannot incorporate the perspective of other people into their judgments. If they want to partake of sexual activity, they assume their partners desire the same. It does not cross their minds that their partners might think differently. The increase in sexually transmitted diseases (STDs) and pregnancies seen in the early adolescent years is ample evidence of reproductive ability wedded to poor cognitive and social skills.

Knowing that puberty begins earlier than in the past and that many adolescents have not developed strong cognitive and interpersonal skills, how far should camps go in trying to control teen sexual behavior? The bottom line is that, even if parents or camp directors are displeased with sexual activity between teenagers, they have limited legal recourse. **State laws protect the right of teenagers to have *consensual* sexual contact with peers close in age.** The age range for sexual activity between peers differs from state to state. Some states allow a two-year difference in age, while others allow a greater age difference, and some states are quite specific about which sexual acts are allowed or forbidden.

Laws continue to change to reflect the changing status of adolescents in society. As camp director, it is up to you to learn about the laws governing the state in which your camp is located and to keep abreast of changes. You can turn to the local district attorney's office to obtain this information.

Directors and staff may be aghast to learn that two teenage campers have managed to depart their cabins in the middle of the night for a private sexual encounter. The reality, though, is that, in the absence of any coercion, the teens have broken no law and the behavior is psychologically normative. Thus teenage sexuality in camps presents the same problem as childhood sexuality. The director must craft a proper response that takes into account the acceptance of the behavior as well as the possible displeasure of parents, staff, and maybe even the camp director him- or herself.

It is sobering to realize how little influence camp directors have over the sexual activity of camp participants. Children experiment with other children. Staff form romantic relationships. Campers form romantic couples. Many participate in sexual play, and some go on to have sexual intercourse. The one positive note is that most sexual activity occurring in camps is not against the law.

*Signs of sexual activity and secrecy
between people of unequal status should
raise a red flag.*

7

Child Sexual Abuse

We purposely address the topic of child sexual abuse last in this book. We do this not because the subject lacks importance, because it does have severe consequences for both camps and individuals. In fact, next to the death of a camper, child molestation is probably a camp director's greatest fear. We address child sexual abuse last because it has received much attention at the expense of other problem sexual behaviors.

Directors know to watch for warning signs, or "red flags," that an adult may be sexually abusing a child. Vigilant for any and all signs of child molesting, these same directors may fail to notice sexual harassment among staff, the victimization of a child by another child, or the escalation of violence in a relationship. Even the most overt signs of these other problematic sexual behaviors may never reach conscious awareness. Either the thoughts are "blocked" because they cause discomfort, or directors simply do not know what to look for or do not recognize the signs when they see them.

Not Just "Stranger Danger"

Just what are the "red flags" that signal child sexual abuse? Camp directors are taught to look for the "evidence" of a male who instantly bonds to children, appears to spend an inordinate amount of time with children, and has poor social skills or is uncomfortable with adults. All this could be true—but it is also not true in many instances. In my clinical practice, I have encountered adult males who molested children yet had impeccable social skills and were actually quite gregarious.

The image of the child molester taught to camp directors, and subsequently to their staff in innumerable trainings, is incomplete:

> Until recently, the public generally thought of "stranger danger" only when worrying about the occurrence of child sexual abuse. A molester was assumed to be a single male who was easily identified by his "seedy" looks and unshaven appearance. He would lurk in shadows and grab children. He was called the "bogeyman" by some and a "pervert" by all. Other commonly held misconceived ideas were that the sex offender was visibly insane, mentally retarded, brutal, depraved, immoral, or oversexed.

He was assumed to be a fiend and to spend time reading or viewing pornography, and he was either an alcoholic or a drug addict. Such popular misconceptions contributed to the belief that the sex offender was somehow not an ordinary person, was easily distinguishable, and always male" (van Dam, 2001, p. 81).

In addition, the focus on adult perpetrators masks the fact that almost 40 percent of offenses against children are perpetrated by individuals aged eighteen and under (Trivits & Reppucci, 2002). While camp directors are on the lookout for adult offenders, they are missing the sexual abuse of campers at the hands of peers, older campers, and the youngest staff members.

A point of confusion among staff is just what constitutes "child sexual abuse." Most people assume that it means a child is touched or penetrated by an adult or forced to perform a sexual act on an adult. But what if there is no physical contact between victim and perpetrator? At least two examples have come to my attention. A seventeen-year-old counselor was fired for sharing intimate details of his sex life with his cabin in response to the campers' repeated requests for general information on sex. No contact occurred between the counselor and the boys. Certainly the sharing of intimate sexual details was against the camp's policies, but the worried camp director referred to the incident as "sexual abuse." In the second example, a foreign staff member undressed in his cabin with his campers after the afternoon swim. One child returned home and mentioned the incident to his parents. They immediately contacted the camp director and wanted the young man fired for exposure. Was this a case of child sexual abuse or of over-reactive parents?

In the legal system, too, incidents of child sexual abuse come to light that involve no contact at all between victim and perpetrator. It is often difficult for a camp director to decide whether abuse has occurred, and this lack of clarity causes confusion as to whether the director should intervene. To shed some light on the confusion surrounding child sexual abuse, we provide here some essential definitions and descriptions.

Pedophilia

I once attended a camp conference where the speaker referred several times to the dangers of the pedophile—a person with the condition of pedophilia—in camps. In fact, the speaker claimed that camp environments were naturally inviting for pedophiles. By the time the session was over, the participants imagined that pedophiles were insidiously infiltrating each and every camp represented there that day. I agree with the speaker that an *active* pedophile would be a nightmarish occurrence for a camp. Fortunately, despite the near hysteria one hears from time to time, pedophiles in camps are a rare occurrence. Other groups pose a far greater risk to the sexual safety of campers than the "bogeyman" pedophile.

What exactly is a pedophile? A commonly held definition is that a pedophile is an individual who has sex with children, but this definition is not precise. As defined in the American Psychiatric Association's classification system of mental disorders,

a pedophile is a person who is sexually aroused by prepubescent children. A diagnosis of pedophilia is made when these conditions are met:

- Over a period of at least six months, recurrent, intense, sexually arousing fantasies, sexual urges, or behaviors involving sexual activity with a prepubescent child or children (generally age thirteen years or younger).

- The person has acted on these sexual urges, or the sexual urges or fantasies cause marked distress or interpersonal difficulty.

- The person is at least sixteen years and at least five years older than the prepubescent child or children.[*]

According to these widely accepted diagnostic criteria, it is possible to be a pedophile yet not have sexual contact with children. Distressing fantasies are enough to warrant the diagnosis. "Clinicians might see patients with pedophilia who have interacted sexually with children, who have only looked at sexualized pictures of children, or have not in any way acted upon their urges but seek treatment because of distress and shame about having such feelings" (Fagan, Wise, Schmidt, & Berlin, 2002, p. 2461–2462).

We can speculate on the implications of the diagnostic criteria for pedophilia in hiring. Do sexual fantasies merit consideration in hiring? If a prospective staffer admits to having sexual fantasies about prepubescent children but has never acted upon them, does this destroy all opportunity to work at a camp? A knee-jerk response would be to deny this person employment. But consider that older campers are often objects of sexual fantasy for staff also. It is not uncommon for staff to be aroused by teenagers. In fact, the majority of adult males easily find themselves sexually attracted to teenagers. How would hiring the person affect camp safety if their sexual fantasies about prepubescent children or teenagers were never acted upon? Though I can offer no evidence to support or refute this contention, it is possible that camps have hired at least a few pedophiles who have not acted on their sexual urges.

Keep in mind that **pedophilia is a psychiatric disorder, not a choice**. This was clearly demonstrated to me in a clinical case. The municipal court system referred seventeen-year-old Robert to my facility for attempting to anally penetrate a six-year-old boy. Robert was a top scholar in his high school as well as a star athlete in the local sports scene. Far from being a loner with poor social skills, Robert was on the surface a model citizen. What's more, he was dating and engaging in consensual sexual activity with a young woman his age. He claimed that the penetration incident was the result of a sudden flashback to his own sexual abuse at the hands of a stranger more than eleven years before. Robert would not veer from this story and was adamant that this was the sole cause for his offense. As a clinician, I found much lacking in his explanation but knew better than to push too quickly. Several months into treatment, an incident occurred that led treatment in a very different direction: Robert's mother found that he was visiting child pornographic sites on the Internet.

---

[*]Reprinted with permission from the *Diagnostic and Statistical Manual of Mental Disorders,* Fourth Edition. Copyright 2000 American Psychiatric Association.

Robert denied all knowledge of the child pornographic sites. However, since he lived alone with his mother, there was no other sensible explanation. After several weeks of my persistent exploration, Robert was finally able to honestly discuss the sexual abuse of the child that had brought him into contact with the law and this treatment. Though he was having sexual relations with his girlfriend, Robert felt most attracted to male prepubescent children. This interest dated back to his own prepubescent days. He was able to admit, with great discomfort, that he masturbated several times a week to fantasies of male children.

Robert was not gay, he felt no attraction to male peers or those older than himself, and he could achieve orgasm with a female. Yet his major focus of sexual arousal was prepubescent males. Robert was not happy with his sexual arousal pattern and was clearly able to see the complications it would cause throughout his life. No doubt there were reasons that might explain Robert's sexual interest in children, but these were far less important than the observation that his sexual preference was not a choice. He had the choice whether to act on his urges, but no choice in his actual preference. Like the popular, outgoing, and actively dating Robert, the majority of pedophiles are not recognizable as having this sexual preference.

My experience with clients and peers suggests that children who have been sexually abused at camps are more often victims of older teenagers than of mature adults. Most of these cases are not reported until years later, long after the victim experienced the abuse. Recall the general finding that 40 percent of incidents of child sexual abuse are perpetrated by adolescents.

Because sexual offenders against children are a varied group, listing specific characteristics of pedophiles is a challenging task. We know that most pedophiles begin offending in the middle to late teen years. They may be aware that they are victimizing a child but fabricate a complicated pseudo-intimate relationship with the child in their own minds. In these situations, offenders believe they are involved in a mutually consensual relationship with the child from which both derive pleasure. Female pedophiles are particularly known for investing time and effort in establishing caring, protective relationships with victims prior to any abuse. These offenders do not perceive of themselves as sexual victimizers but rather as concerned, caring, even loving friends and confidants. Adult and teenage pedophiles alike are just as capable of these rationalizations.

Child Molestation

A pedophile may never act out sexual fantasies. In contrast, by definition **a child molester is someone who has sexual contact with children**. We will use the word "molester" to refer to any teen or adult who has sexual contact with a child, whether due to pedophilia or not.

Why would a teen or adult who is not sexually attracted to children initiate sex with a child? The research literature is quite helpful here. We pointed out earlier that males are sexually aroused by a great array of stimuli, apparently including children. Researchers make much of the finding that a fair percentage of "normal" males experience some form of molestation fantasy. Here are some of their other findings:

- Between 21 and 35 percent of the male population does not consider sex with children to be problematic (van Dam, 2001).

- A significant minority of male university students partially endorsed statements such as "Many children would like to have sex with an adult once they tried it" (Briere, 1992).

- In a study of male erotic fantasies, 61.7 percent fantasized about a sexual encounter with a young girl, and 3.2 percent fantasized about such an encounter with a young boy (Crepault & Couture, 1980).

- In a study of male undergraduate students, 21 percent reported being attracted to children, while 9 percent fantasized about actual sexual contact with a child (Briere & Runtz, 1989).

In these studies, sexual contact did not refer specifically to physical contact. The males in these studies were also aroused by fantasies of exposing themselves to children, watching children undress or perform other personal acts, and "talking dirty" to them.

At the beginning of this chapter, we told of a counselor who shared personal sexual information with his campers. Was this a lapse of judgment or was he achieving sexual arousal from the involvement? What about the counselor who got into trouble for undressing in front of his group of campers? Was this, too, a lapse in judgment or a source of sexual gratification? The answers are bound to elude us, but we know for certain that males, in particular, may be sexually stimulated by a wide variety of specific interactions with children. Thankfully, even in situations where such sexual arousal does occur, males typically do not act on it.

Sexual attraction to children can be viewed as falling along a continuum. One pole represents sexual interest only in prepubescent children; the other represents no sexual interest in children at all. Between these extremes we find a range of degrees of interest in prepubescent children. In regard to teenagers, research shows that most adults are easily attracted to youth who have entered puberty. A continuum illustrating adult sexual attraction to adolescents would show a much smaller range than that for prepubescent children, and most adults would fall at the end that indicates a fair amount of sexual arousal. Again, this pertains mostly to adult males. Many males will be sexually aroused by children, especially female children, but most will never go past the point of fantasy, and few will ever attempt a sexual act with a child.

Why does an adult go past the point of fantasy and actually make sexual contact with a child? **People who are not able to gratify their sexual needs in mature mutual encounters may fall back on children for such gratification.** In clinical experience, my peers and I find that adults and teenagers referred for having sexual contact with prepubescent children did so because other sexual outlets were not available. Of course some had pedophilic interests, but the majority sought involvement in mutual relationships but were unable to connect. The variety of reasons for this includes weak social skills, not meeting the generally accepted criteria for attractiveness, and excessive timidity. There is never one sole reason why a person initiates sexual activity with a child, but lack of access to other outlets often plays a role.

Unlike pedophiles, child molesters may be motivated by factors having nothing to do with sexual urges. An adult may sexually abuse a child as a means of exhibiting power or status, or as a method of hurting another person. My clinical peers and I have noted that underlying sibling incest is often the wish to retaliate against a parent. The child cannot hurt the parent directly so avenges him- or herself through aggressive sexual contact with a sibling.

All in all, a pedophile is motivated by a deviant arousal pattern, while a molester can be motivated by non-sexual as well as sexual means. The fact that the motivation may be non-sexual in no way decreases the severity of the offense, nor does it keep us from defining an incident of molestation as a sexual offense.

No "official" criteria have been developed to determine whether someone is a child molester. Camp directors can use the following definition of sexual abuse formulated by Carla van Dam (2001). According to van Dam, an adult has committed an act of child molestation if the act meets three criteria:

- **There is violation of a trusting relationship with unequal power and/or unequal advanced knowledge.** The perpetrator is an older individual and thus has more status, power, and knowledge than the child.

- **There is a need for secrecy.** The perpetrator not only does not reveal the activity to peers but also cajoles, threatens, or bribes the victim into silence. The perpetrator may also keep sexual interests and motivations a secret—for example, furtively watching children shower or change, or undressing in front of campers under the guise of necessity.

- **Some form of sexual activity has occurred.** This criterion encompasses all forms of sexual activity, ranging from non-contact offenses to actual intercourse.

Van Dam's criteria acknowledge that most incidents of child molestation involve people who already know each other. Cases of molestation in which strangers victimize children are rare. No camp director has ever told me of a staff member initiating sexual contact with a camper with whom he or she did not already have some form of relationship. Even among clinical cases, the victims were family members, the children of friends, or other children who were somehow under their care. Parents warn their children to be wary of strangers, but the risk of molestation is far greater from a person with whom a child already has a relationship. This is why van Dam does not include stranger molestation in her definition. Such incidents are rare, and there is no reason to think they would be any more frequent in camps.

Applying the criteria to a non-camp example, van Dam described an incident in which a high school football coach created a peephole into the male shower room and proceeded to masturbate while he secretly watched his male students shower. In this case, all criteria were met: a difference in status (the coach clearly had more power than the victims), secrecy was inherent in the act, and sexual activity occurred.

In a camp example, a male counselor arranged a nude swim for the boys in his cabin. This occurred at a small pond some distance from camp. Prior to departing, he informed his unit leader that he was taking his campers for an early morning run. Afterwards, he told the campers not to mention the activity as he might get in trouble.

On the surface, the nude swim with campers might simply have reflected the counselor's bad judgment rather than ill intent. But by referring to van Dam's three criteria, we see the more problematic nature of the incident. First, unequal power was evident. Second, the event was performed secretly. The staff member purposely misinformed his unit leader and also told his campers not to tell anybody else about the event. Finally, a sexual act occurred. It did not involved physical contact, but exposure of one's genitals would classify as a sexual occurrence.

In fact, about a week after this incident, one camper told another staff member about the secret swim, and the perpetrator was terminated. Two years later this same man was court-mandated to treatment after arrest for exposure in a non-camp incident. Apparently he was an exhibitionist, a person who derives sexual satisfaction from exposing himself.

Grooming the Victim and Caretakers

The underlying goal for a molester is to obtain sexual gratification from a child without being caught. To simply walk into the household of another adult and offend against a child would be far too risky, so molesters formulate ways to achieve the object of their desire while minimizing negative outcomes. Clinicians who work with child molesters are often struck by the similarities of their methods. Some have learned their "techniques" through direct education by other molesters—for example, through Internet sites or literature geared to this population—but most develop their repertoire on their own. The treatment field has borrowed the word *grooming* to describe these very similar techniques.

Grooming refers to the process of desensitizing the victim to abuse. An offender could simply drug a child into submission, and this does indeed occur, but the more common process is to establish a relationship with a child and gradually increase the amount of physical contact that occurs. The child may receive gifts, compliments, or special treatment from the molester as an initial way of establishing trust. The next step is non-sexual physical touch such as would occur during playful roughhousing and wrestling. Then there is brief contact with the genital region. This genital contact occurs with increasing frequency and for longer periods of time. All the while, the child is still treated to special privileges that further bind him or her emotionally to the molester.

The grooming process can take quite a long time to complete successfully. Camp directors can be reassured that it would be statistically rare for a staff member to molest a child on the first few nights of an encampment. A staff member will wait until a relationship of trust has been established before attempting sexual contact; this could take days to weeks to occur. Molesters operate methodically to gain the trust, cooperation, and ultimately the silence of victims.

Researchers have various ideas of how grooming proceeds. Most agree, though, that molesters also groom other adults in a child's life to minimize the chance of detection. If parents trust the molester and believe that he or she has only the purest motives in establishing a relationship with their child, they will grant the molester more time alone with the child and question the child less, if at all, about any harm that might be occurring. For just this reason, camp directors are warned to watch for staff who appear "too good to be true" in their interactions with children. A staff member who behaves impeccably and seems completely upfront in dealings with kids probably does not have hidden motives, but directors need to know that **a molester will seek to establish a veneer of model citizenship so as to avoid getting caught**. Lulling other adults into complacency is essential for the molester's success. In this way, the molester gains power not only over the child but also over the child's caretakers.

What to Do?

Of all the problem sexual behaviors we have cited in this book, child molestation is the most difficult to combat because it is the most secretive of the abuses. Offenders are certain not to reveal their activities, and, in almost all cases, their victims also do not report their victimization. Camp sessions that last only one or two weeks do not give staff enough time to identify behavioral changes that might occur after an episode of molestation. In many encounters, though, no behavioral change will be evident. In fact, child victims often do not know they are victims. An offender may expose himself under the pretense of changing for a swim, or furtively watch children undress, or grope a child's genitals "accidentally" while roughhousing.

Research suggests that one way to successfully prevent most child molestation is to identify pedophiles and keep them away from children. Unfortunately, this strategy does not work even for the best equipped clinics, let alone camps. How exactly does one identify a pedophile? It is here that the plan falls apart.

The research literature clearly shows that it is next to impossible to predict who will be a perpetrator of inappropriate sexual acts. This book has challenged several times the ability of a camp director to identify child molesters, sexually aggressive partners, and sexually aggressive children *before* an incident occurs. *Forensic Evaluation of Juveniles* (Grisso, 1998), a text written for the juvenile justice field, directs clinicians to evaluate all these factors in determining a youth's risk for violent behaviors: chronicity, recency, severity and frequency of past violent behaviors, substance use, peers, history of family conflict, neglect, abuse, history of family legal involvement, personality traits, and mental disorders. How many camp employment interviews or camper screenings come close to such a thorough evaluation of potentially problematic individuals?

Another clinically oriented guide, *Assessing Men Who Sexually Abuse* (Briggs, Doyle, Gooch, & Kennington, 1998), calls for a thorough assessment of sexual arousal and fantasies, history of romantic relationships, personal victimization, self-esteem, empathy, substance use, sexual knowledge, and patterns of distorted thinking. Again, just how accomplished are camp directors in gathering such information in the interview process?

No director can elicit a detailed sexual history from each person who interviews for employment or seeks placement in a camp. Most parents and staffers know better than to present such details. I doubt that any of you will ever encounter a prospective employee who admits during an interview that he or she is a pedophile. If you are fortunate enough to learn of this tendency during an interview, or if a background check shows that the interviewee was involved in a previous offense against a child, by all means refuse this person employment. Just don't count on this information being available.

Given the reality that camp directors will find out about child molestation either not at all or only *after* incidents have occurred, what can you do? You must be prepared to intervene when you suspect child abuse, but you can also take steps to keep molesters from feeling at home in your camp.

Response to Reports of Staff / Camper Sexual Contact

A report of sexual contact between a staff member and a child is the nightmare that camp directors hope never to have. Child molestation is a felony and must be treated accordingly. Intervene if you have even the slightest inkling that molestation is occurring in your camp.

While it is essential to intervene immediately in a child molestation incident, there is a limit to what you can do. A report of child sex abuse falls under the authority of the criminal justice system for investigation and, if warranted, prosecution. Those found guilty of the offense serve prison time, are placed into a sex offender registry, are required to attend treatment, and may even be mandated to notify those in the neighborhood of their crime.

Upon receiving a report of child molestation, you have these basic goals:

1. Protect the child from further harm.

Tell the child that immediate steps will be taken to stop the abuse. Stay calm—the child will monitor your reactions.

2. Offer the child comfort.

Listen and demonstrate to the child that you are taking the report very seriously. Let the child know that he/she did the right thing in informing the director about the abuse. Assure the child that he/she did nothing wrong.

3. Contact the police or child protection agency to initiate an investigation.

Many camp directors instinctively assume the role of private investigator in these cases. Don't do it. Leave this to the professionals. One thing that we have learned over the last two decades is that great care must be taken in both preparing and performing interviews with possible victims of child sexual abuse. Such interviewing is not a skill that the majority of camp directors are familiar with let alone have practiced. Question the child only about the most basic information—who? when? where? what happened?—and share this with the local authorities.

Call the authorities even if you have some doubts about the truth of a story. Some cases will present undeniable evidence of molestation, but many others will boil down to a "he said/she said" situation. As with sexual assault, you can let the legal system determine guilt or innocence.

If molestation is perpetrated by an older camper—for example, a teenage camper molests a younger child—you should still contact the authorities. Forced sexual activity is a crime whether the offender is an adult or a juvenile.

Inform the accused only when the police request his/her presence.

It is important that you contact the local authorities before the season even begins, to learn of the protocol for dealing with an incident of molestation. For example:

- Do the local authorities want parents present during an interview?

- Should parents talk to children before the authorities do?

- What is the protocol if the accused staff member is also a minor? In this case, a representative may need to be present before an official interview begins. Citing the example of my own state of Pennsylvania, in cases of child molestation, I must contact both the police and the state child-abuse hotline. This results in two different investigations: a criminal investigation and a child safety investigation. The local authorities can question the victim without the parents present but cannot question an accused minor without their presence.

4. Notify the parents of the victim and the parents of a juvenile offender.

Such phone calls are by no means easy or pleasant. Parents of the offending teenager may request—or even demand—that no police be involved. However, parents should already be aware of the camp's policy on involving the police. Dependent on local protocol, police or child protection agents may wish to have parents present for the interview.

I find it interesting that, among the hundreds of camp brochures I have seen, I have never once seen it stated that "If your child seriously harms another camp participant, our policy is to contact the police." Granted, placing such a statement in a brochure could puzzle or worry a prospective parent by suggesting that the camp has safety issues. My position is that camps do have safety issues and should not perpetuate misconceptions by trying to hide the potential dangers of attending camp. We do not hesitate to describe our emergency medical procedures because parents can accept that medical emergencies sometimes occur in camps. Parents are far less accepting of the idea that a staff member or another camper could intentionally hurt their child, but we know it sometimes happens. We have a responsibility to let parents and campers know that we take their safety seriously and will implement every safety measure available.

5. Find out your legal rights and obligations.

If the formal investigation concludes that child sexual abuse may have occurred, the accused is suspended from further duty until the criminal justice system makes its judgment. If you believe this staff member is an immediate threat to another camper, this person must be placed in a containment area. Serious acts warrant immediate termination.

Consult your camp's legal representative to determine the proper procedure for dealing with the accused staff member. For example:

- Do you fire a staff member based on an accusation alone?

- Do you suspend the person until a legal ruling is handed down?

- Do you send the accused child home?

In most cases, you must remove the accused from childcare duties. One camp kept a male group leader who was accused of making sexual contact with a counselor-in-training more than twenty years his younger. The accused was placed on kitchen duty and was forbidden any unsupervised contact with children. In this situation, the director made the right decision, as the charges were eventually dropped against the staff member. Other directors would never have allowed the person to remain on camp property. There is no one correct answer to this dilemma.

Keeping Alert for Red Flags

We turn now to the things you can do to prevent child molesters from taking advantage of your camp's easy access to children. Most camp directors are already inundated with information on indicators of molestation, so I will review them only briefly. The work of many organizations that serve children suggests that you keep an eye on:

- Individuals who develop a special one-on-one relationship with a child.

- Individuals who spend time alone with children.

Since most molestation at camp requires a grooming period for both the victim and the camp administration, the probability is low that any molestation could occur early in the session. This gives camp directors time to monitor for telltale signs. Based on the information covered in this chapter, **any sign of sexual activity and secrecy among individuals of unequal status should raise a red flag**. Two incidents illustrate how to interpret these signs.

Counselor John allowed his cabin of nine-year-old boys to have a mud-wrestling tournament in the camp wetland. John allowed some of the children to perform this activity with no clothes on. When they returned to camp, both he and the children told others of the tournament. The camp director was alarmed and explained to John that this was not an appropriate activity in this camp. John made no effort to conceal the event and apologized for this infraction.

Counselor Mark staged a similar tournament with his campers but, before returning to camp, he made all the children promise never to tell anyone of the event. Why did Mark feel the need for secrecy? The event does not brand Mark as a definite child molester, but the combination of secrecy and sexuality between those with different power and status should raise a red flag.

Recall the incident in which a counselor took his campers for a nude swim under the guise of an early morning run. The only reason the director learned of this was that one of the campers let the information slip to another staff member. The amount of effort this camper put into attempting to cover up his disclosure was especially revealing. The entire cabin, including the counselor in question, had made a vow to keep the activity a secret. So much effort surrounding even slightly questionable sexual behavior between individuals of unequal status certainly warrants investigation.

Traits to Look For

In her excellent book, *Identifying Child Molesters,* van Dam (2001) offers a list of traits identifying those who may pose a sexual risk to children. In van Dam's view, several criteria must be met before we can assume that a molester is in our midst.

1. **The individual:**
is exceptionally charming and/or helpful

To successfully groom both a victim and the camp community, the molester must obtain the trust of all participants. Through excessive charm and helpfulness, the molester establishes a positive and responsible image. Many charming, helpful people are certainly not child molesters. This is why this first trait must occur in combination with a second set of traits.

2. **The individual:**
   engages in peerlike play
   prefers the company of children
   roughhouses with and tickles children
   obtains immediate "insider" status

An individual who is exceptionally charming and helpful and also engages in peerlike play, prefers the company of children, roughhouses with children, and gains immediate insider status with children should be considered a possible danger. Molesters are often able to establish instant relationships with children. They are attuned to children and can quickly engage with them at their developmental level. Van Dam believes that charm and/or helpfulness in combination with just one of these four characteristics should be sufficient information to make a director wary. The person displaying such traits must be thoroughly monitored.

3. **The individual:**
   fails to honor clear boundaries
   goes on the offensive

Van Dam writes that if either of these last two traits occurs in combination with the first two sets of traits, this is sufficient reason to exclude that person from any further involvement with campers.

Molesters will often simply disregard camp policy and rules. If the staff member does not stop a questionable behavior when asked, this is a serious concern. For example, if a staff member has been found alone in a cabin with a child and is told not to do it again but then repeats the act, this is a failure to honor a specified boundary. In combination with the first two sets of traits, we might consider this an offense worthy of termination.

If the individual becomes defensive over questions about his or her behavior, this is indeed a warning sign. I concur completely with van Dam in this appraisal. We have both encountered molesters who, when questioned about their activities, go to great lengths to protect their image, including putting down the victim, the legal system, and even on occasion ourselves. Van Dam cites an example of a male, later convicted of child molestation, who threatened a libel suit against parents who made an accusation against him.

While some researchers have explored the characteristics of sexual offenders, others have explored the characteristics of victims. Not all children at camp are equally targeted by molesters. Some children are more vulnerable than others to sexual abuse because they exhibit traits and characteristics that molesters find more inviting. These children often lack confidence, have low self-esteem, are lonely, have little adult support, and have a need for attention. Children with poor verbal skills due to age or some type of disability are also more appealing as they have limited ability to inform others of the sexual activity. Children who are especially attractive also are more likely to win a molester's attention. Recognition of a growing relationship between a suspicious staff member and a child exhibiting any of these characteristics should prompt an immediate investigation of the situation.

One additional step is necessary before we can say we have taken every precaution for the protection of our campers. We need to be certain that our camp environment is not hospitable to child molesters. We know that certain characteristics make families more prone to child molestation. Molesters look for families with poor boundaries and high levels of stress. The molester's interest in a child is often welcomed by overburdened parents who have little time to spend with the child. Indeed, some molesters purposely date—and even marry—single parents simply to gain access to their children. In contrast, a molester will want little to do with a family that has clear boundaries, talks openly about sex, and shows the child love and support.

Just as some family environments are more conducive to molestation, camp environments may be more or less conducive to such abuse. In Chapter 3, we noted that problem sexual behaviors are more likely to thrive in camps that tolerate bullying, abusive management practices, lax security measures, and high levels of staff stress. The camp that actively addresses such sexual safety issues signals to potential molesters that the secret encounters they desire will not remain secret. The best defense is a camp culture that creates doubt in the minds of molesters that they can get away with it.

*Camps cannot stamp out sex, but they
can minimize harmful sexual activity.*

8

Camp Sexual Safety Plan

In a newly published book on camp management, I encountered a list of recommendations for all camps. The very first item on the list was the SAD rule: "No Sex, no Alcohol, and no Drugs on camp property." How realistic is this? Now that mandatory random drug testing is available, we have a fighting chance of achieving no alcohol and no drugs, but what chance do we have of achieving no sex? As I hope this book has made clear, no camp can hope to successfully stamp out all sexual behavior.

As an alternative to the SAD rule, I offer an approach that has taken hold in many industries: *harm reduction*. The concept of harm reduction is borrowed from the field of drug and alcohol treatment, where practitioners have come to grips with the reality that a great number of substance abusers are simply not going to stop using drugs. Rather than giving up on hardcore drug users and focusing efforts on more casual users who may derive more benefit from treatment, providers have opted to help hardcore users by reducing the harm of their addiction.

For example, heroin addicts risk numerous dangers, including overdose, but they can benefit from education on safe drug use. They can take part in a needle exchange program to minimize exposure to common intravenous drug-use infections, most notably HIV. They can also benefit by using medications that lessen their drug cravings. Although a harm reduction protocol like this does not stop drug use, it does reduce drug use, and it averts some of the costly consequences.

Reducing Harmful Sexual Behavior in Camps

A harm-reduction approach to sexual behavior seeks to minimize harmful sexual activity rather than to eradicate all sex from camps. Camp administrators tend to take for granted that stamping out sex is part of their job. I think back to my first season as a program director, where one of my duties was to perform staff bed checks at some point during the night. The female program director would perform the same activity on the girls' side of the camp. If a staff member was not in bed, we left a note on the pillow instructing the individual to see the camp director in the morning. Most nights, we found all staff members in their beds. On those few occasions when we didn't, the culprits received written warnings from the director before breakfast.

In retrospect, I wonder just what we were doing. Nobody was ever fired. My female colleague and I were sleep-deprived each day from checking the beds of more than seventy people each and every night. We certainly didn't stop sexual activity. Numerous sexual relationships still occurred—the couples simply got better at eluding detection. Yet the director insisted on this nightly scrutiny, seeing it as a necessity that no sex should occur in camp. The director's goal might have been laudable for its sincerity and for the tenacity with which he pursued it. But it was also a waste of scarce time and resources.

Our challenge is to move past this sort of unquestioning acceptance that sexual activity must not happen in camps, to a more realistic appraisal of its occurrence. Instead of devoting our resources to interventions with no inherent validity—bed checks, rules outlawing sexual activity, the infamous first-night sex talk—we can take the more sensible approach of trying to reduce the harm of sex. With a harm-reduction perspective, our job is not to stop all sex, which we have learned we cannot do. Rather, our job is to make our camps as safe as possible for all participants by striving to protect individuals from harmful and unwelcome sexual activity. The following interventions are a natural outgrowth of a harm-reduction approach.

Along with taking steps to reduce harm, I urge you to retain legal counsel. Each camp should have a legal representative to field questions and help resolve issues. You should never attempt to handle the report of a serious incident such as sexual assault completely on your own. You want to be certain that a well-meaning intervention does not later turn into a legal problem. In particular, the laws on sexual harassment are becoming more refined as more and more sexual harassment disputes are heard in the courts. You certainly do not want your camp to be branded with a sexual harassment lawsuit.

Harm Reduction with Staff

When faced with an accusation of inappropriate sexual behavior by staff, camp directors tend to adopt two contrasting responses. They either fire the accused, who may in fact be innocent of the charges; or they minimize the incident, such as telling the accused not to do it again, then putting him or her back into the camp community—the proverbial "slap on the wrist."

Both responses affect the entire camp community. In the intimate camp environment, news of inappropriate sexual activity spreads like wildfire. An immediate termination risks a reputation of unfairness for the director. A light punishment, on the other hand, shows staff that the camp director does not take the issue of safety seriously. If one staff member can be sexually inappropriate without repercussions, what else will staff members get away with?

A response more helpful to all involved—the camp administration, the victim, the accused, and other camp staff—is to create a shared understanding of what constitutes harmful sexual activity and how the camp will investigate such allegations. This has already been touched on in the chapters on sexual assault and sexual harassment. To simply state that all sexual activity is inappropriate and unwelcome at camp, as in the

"SAD rule," is not enough. We need to take more realistic steps to ensure the safety of camp staff.

The following guidelines embody a comprehensive approach to harm reduction among camp staff.

1. Formulate a harassment policy and teach it to staff.

A sexual harassment policy is the main girder of a harm-reduction approach. Such a policy is no longer just an option for any business. Indeed, the presence of such a policy is the very first factor a court will examine in determining the liability of a workplace in a harassment suit. A harassment policy does not forbid all sexual activity. Instead, it acknowledges that sexuality is part of the workplace and that some of this activity may be unwelcome. If your camp does not have a sexual harassment policy in place, your first order of business should be to create one. Some guidelines are presented in Chapter 6.

I recommend that the general harassment and sexual harassment policies be combined in a single document. The document should specify that camp administration will take action against any employee whose behavior negatively affects the well-being of another employee. The sample harassment policy shown on page 130 encompasses both sexual harassment issues.

2. Create a policy restricting romantic relationships between supervisors and supervisees.

The rationale for this policy was discussed in Chapter 5 in connection with quid pro quo sexual harassment. Of all staff romantic relationships, those between supervisors and supervisees have the most potential for damage. Supervisors must know that, if they do become involved with a supervisee, they risk demotion, a change of position, or termination.

3. Formulate a staff sexual behavior policy.

This policy covers the expression of normative sexual behavior around campers. The aim is to ensure that staff model appropriate sexual behavior for the camp and do not stray into activities that could cause harm. Topics for this policy include:

- **Dress code.** What clothing is considered risqué?

- **Displays of affection.** Are staff allowed to hold hands in public? Kiss? Visit each others' cabins?

- **Inappropriate sex talk.** Warn staff against discussing their romantic pursuits with campers. Such talk could be the basis for a lawsuit.

Camp ABC Harassment Policy

All employees have the right to work in an environment free of harassment. It is the responsibility of each manager to create and maintain such an environment. In addition, it is the responsibility of each employee to respect the rights of co-workers.

Employees are NOT permitted to harass other employees. Harassment results in an offensive and/or hostile working environment. Harassment can consist of both sexual and non-sexual behaviors including:

public humiliation
mockery
disrespectful treatment
assault and other unwanted
   physical contact
intimidation
threats
cruel or inappropriate practical jokes
destruction of personal property
leering
wolf whistles
discussion of another's sexual
   attributes and/or inadequacies

sexual innuendo
lewd and/or threatening letters
displays of pornography
pressure for dates or sexual activity
sexually explicit gestures
unwelcome touching and hugging
sabotaging another person's work
sexist and/or insulting graffiti
inappropriate invitations
hostile put-downs

This list is not comprehensive. Other behaviors may be determined as unwelcome and thus harassing.

An employee who experiences harassment should tell the perpetrator to stop and that further advances or displays of similar behavior are unwelcome. The employee should inform the camp director immediately:

- If the perpetrator is a supervisor.

- If the harassment continues.

- If the employee feels unsafe.

An investigation will be conducted discretely. Because of the personal and sensitive nature of harassment complaints, the nature of the complaint shall be provided on a need-to-know basis only. Should the investigation determine that an individual has harassed another employee, disciplinary action up to and including discharge will be taken against the offender.

Camp ABC prohibits any form of retaliation against an employee for filing a complaint under this policy or for providing assistance in the investigation of a complaint.

As you can see, this combination of policies—sexual harassment, general harassment, supervisor/supervisee relationships, and sexual behavior—stipulates protection for all staff from unwelcome behavior, whether sexual or non-sexual in nature. In addition, the policies lay the foundation of a sexual safety plan for the camp. They do not condemn sexual activity among staff but clearly state that any sexual activity that occurs must remain within defined limits.

4. Formulate a protocol for reporting sexual assault or harassment.

The camp's response to serious sexual offenses should come as no surprise. Staff should be informed, both in writing and during orientation, what specific procedure will be followed if an incident is reported. The protocol should emphasize these points.

- Make clear the camp's stance on refusing to determine guilt, letting the victim decide on police involvement, and possible consequences.

- The director's obligation is to implement changes that lead to a safer, harassment-free environment. This may or may not entail punishment for the offender, depending on the details of the incident.

- The administration does not dispense relationship therapy but can direct staff to appropriate resources in the community.

- The administration actively seeks out information on unwanted contact, behaviors that might constitute harassment, and factors that interfere with job performance. It does not want to know the details of staff relationships otherwise.

5. Evaluate staff solely on measurable performance characteristics.

Failure to meet performance standards should be the only reason to discipline staff. The fact that they may be involved in a relationship should not enter the equation unless that relationship affects job performance. If adults are in a mutually agreeable relationship that exhibits no harassment, leads to no inappropriate behavior around campers, and does not interfere with job performance, the camp administration does not need to become in any way involved.

If performance suffers as the result of a sexual relationship, the camp administration has a duty to take action. **Staff should be disciplined only for the adverse effects of a sexual relationship on job performance**. If a staff member oversleeps, misses activities, and is less than attentive to children because of a sexual involvement, the director disciplines him or her for poor performance, not for the relationship that is the cause. An assistant director once proudly told me that she fired two instructors because of their camp relationship. For a camp's legal security, it would be better to stick to objective performance measures for disciplinary action. All parties involved may already know that the root cause is the romantic relationship. The director's job is not to stop or fix this relationship but to attend to issues of job performance.

6. Monitor the use of alcohol.

Many incidents of sexual assault occur while one or both parties are under the influence of alcohol. The growing use of random alcohol screening with mandatory consequences for its use will go a long way toward preventing such assaults.

	Staff Harm-Reduction Training
	Discuss the inevitability of romantic and sexual relationships occurring among some staff.
	Discuss camp's philosophy on staff romantic relationships.
	Present harassment policy. • Inform staff whether the policy includes harassment based on sexual orientation. • Discuss types of sexual harassment: quid pro quo, hostile environment.
	Present policy restricting romantic relationships between supervisors and supervisees.
	Present staff sexual behavior policy.
	Present protocol for reporting sexual assault and sexual harassment. • Present appropriate vignettes. • Review camp response to serious offenses.
	Present staff performance evaluations. Have a blank evaluation ready for staff to see.
	Present alcohol and drug use policy. If performing random drug testing, demonstrate on a volunteer.
	Discuss monitoring protocol for above policies.
	Allow time for questions and answers.

Conveying Policies to Staff

The camp administration should provide to each staff member a copy of each policy. It is not enough, however, simply to hand out these policies. The administration must have at least a period of discussion for each policy during staff training. This does not mean giving employees several minutes to read the policies followed by time for questions. Such an indifferent approach suggests that the camp really has no intention of enforcing the policies. **The camp director him- or herself should lead the workshop on these policies.**

The chapters on sexual assault and harassment provide material that can be used in these trainings, and we provide a sample agenda here. To bring the policies to life, I recommend that you have staff members act out vignettes based on true incidents that occurred in the camp (changing the names, of course), on incidents described in this book, or on the unwelcome and offensive behaviors listed on page 72. Assembled staff can then be asked how they would handle each incident.

I suggest that directors discuss policies and issues regarding staff relationships on the very first day of camp. Within the first few minutes of meeting, staff members will have already begun to evaluate each other in terms of sexual interest.

Harm Reduction with Campers

There is no reason to re-invent the wheel in this section. The American Camping Association has innumerable resources on safety issues with children. Available video curricula do an excellent presentation on safety concerns, and a protocol for protecting children from sexual contact with adults is already widely accepted throughout the industry. We offer here some additional harm-reduction approaches that focus on child sexuality and child sexual abuse.

1. Formulate a camp protocol for normative sexual activity.

Before the camp can create any policy for harm-reduction with campers, it must first decide how it will deal with occurrences of normative sexual activity. This may be the most difficult step for camps. We already know how to handle non-normative and aggressive behaviors—often sending the camper home. But what about normative displays?

I am reminded of an example from my early camp staff days. Early one morning a counselor found two male children, clothed just in undergarments, grinding against one another in one of their beds. The incident was brought to the attention of the camp director who proceeded to notify the parents. I can still recall how, several hours later, the parents of one child emerged from their car and proceeded to beat him in front of the collected staff. Did the camp director do any good in reporting this incident to the parents?

All camps must formulate a protocol for handling sexual behaviors. Some camps choose to report all occurrences of sexual activity. Others do not get involved unless the contact is unwelcome or is occurring between campers of widely different ages. How your camp will respond is a decision that has to be made by the current administration, but the topic must definitely be discussed. If the decision is to contact parents or terminate the child from camp for normative displays of sexuality, then campers must be told this at the very first all-camp meeting.

The protocol should **specify that staff who become aware of any sexual activity between campers should bring it to the attention of the administration.** Staff should not be the ones to decide whether campers' sexual liaisons warrant concern. Only the camp director has the authority to make this decision. Chapters 6 and 7 provide guidelines for handling reports of sexual activity involving campers.

2. Write a "safety" letter to parents.

A letter to be signed by parents regarding "hot button" topics such as violence and sex in the camp community is a valuable first step in harm reduction. The letter should request their assistance in minimizing occurrences of harmful behavior. Many camp directors hesitate to ask parents for such help because openly broaching such sensitive areas might make prospective parents wary. My response is that such directors are holding on to the misconceptions, outlined in Chapter 2, that they can offer complete safety to campers, that sex should not occur in camps, and that sex can be prevented in camps. Seeking to avoid bringing sexual issues to the forefront shows more interest in maintaining a positive image for the camp than in promoting camp safety.

The sample parent safety letter provided in the Appendix is adapted from one created by Norman Friedman and William Young for SAFETY underwriters, a division of the A. M. Skier Insurance Company. The letter sets just the right tone of educating and reassuring.

3. Write an "unwelcome touch" letter to parents.

Prevention methods that aim to teach children to say "no" to unwanted physical contact and to inform caregivers of such encounters are fairly new. At the core, they teach children to be more assertive in their interactions with adults. The important question, though, is whether such programs actually work.

Reports indicate that some children are inadvertently harmed by these interventions. Children may become oversensitive to numerous forms of interactions with adults, including completely appropriate ones. Some parents report that their children experience increased anxiety, if not outright fear, after participating in such programs. Conversely—and unexpectedly—other children and families become overconfident after attending the programs. This overconfidence that they are protected from abuse may actually place children at more risk.

Many researches have pointed out obvious flaws in unwelcome touch programs. If sexual abuse occurs, the resulting embarrassment, shame, and conflicted emotions regarding the molester can make it nearly impossible to inform another person. In many instances, children must report the abuse to several different people before they are believed. It is difficult enough to share the details of a sexual offense with just one person, let alone repeatedly sharing details before finding someone who will act on the information. This is especially difficult for the child if the molester is a family member or a close friend of the family.

I do not intend to deride unwelcome touch programs. Although they lack supporting data and have negative effects for some participants, they are an important part of a comprehensive prevention agenda for camps. Many directors have reported being satisfied with such programs. Remember, though, that an unwelcome touch program is only one part of a comprehensive safety program. We should not expect campers to assume the major responsibility to protect themselves from unwanted sexual contact.

The Appendix includes a sample unwelcome touch letter to parents, accompanied by recommendations for teaching children about their private parts. It was written by Norman Friedman of the SAFETY underwriters, a division of the A. M. Skier Insurance Company.

4. Create an "unwelcome behavior" policy for campers.

As the sample policy on page 136 shows, this document is far less formal than the harassment policy for staff. It should be read and discussed on the first night of camp, preferably in individual units. Children can sign it so as to make it more formal in their eyes. This same document can address how children should respond if an adult's behavior makes them uncomfortable. To help campers, especially the younger ones, understand the message, it is helpful for staff to give examples of these activities.

Camp ABC Unwelcome Behavior Policy

All members of Camp ABC have a right to be safe.

We do not allow any behavior that threatens the safety of another camp member. This includes but is not limited to:

- making fun of another person
- unwanted touching of another person
- intimidation
- threats
- cruel practical jokes
- destruction of personal property

It is disrespectful to the opposite sex if we perform any of the following actions:

- leering
- wolf whistles
- discussion of another person's body
- lewd and/or threatening letters
- pornography
- pressure for dates or sexual favors
- sexually explicit gestures
- unwelcome touching and hugging

Any of these behaviors will result in discipline, up to and including being sent home.

Campers have the right to be safe with staff. If any staff member or another camper does something that makes you feel uncomfortable, be sure to tell
_____.

5. Teach staff what to do when they discover sexual activity between campers.

Staff must know that the camp administration is the *only* authority in sexual incidents involving campers. However, you can show them how to respond in non-harmful ways when they encounter such activity. In Chapter 6, we suggested these steps:

- Calmly tell the campers to stop the activity immediately in a non-shaming, non-threatening, non-judgmental way.

- Report the activity to camp administration. The camp director will determine whether coercion was involved and formulate a response based on the details of the case.

As you help staff respond appropriately to sexual incidents, you can make them aware of the camp's philosophy regarding normative sexual activity. I suggest that you present several camper sexual vignettes during staff orientation and have them practice in groups. This activity will evoke laughter for many and discomfort for some, but it is an excellent way to prepare staff for the unexpected encounters they are bound to witness. This preparation will avoid the knee-jerk response that the activity is wrong and needs to be punished and help them formulate less judgmental responses.

6. Create a policy regarding staff/camper contact.

This is one area in which camps far exceed expectations. Staff should be given a written policy covering:

- The camp's position on such issues as appropriate contact, being alone with a child, roughhousing and tickling, and post-season contact. The American Camping Association offers numerous resources for this topic area.

- Their responsibility to report suspicious behavior of fellow staff.

- Camp policy regarding allegations of staff/camper sexual activity.

Following is a sample policy for dealing with such allegations. Before formulating a written policy for your own camp, contact the local police department to find out how they would like you to handle specific incidents. For example, do they want the parents present for the interview, or would they rather meet with the camper alone first? Also contact the camp's legal representative to discuss options for the accused. Can he or she be suspended with pay? Could suspending the person for an allegation result in possible legal repercussions for the camp?

Conveying Policies to Staff

A staff training focused on harm reduction with campers should be held on the second day of camp, after the training on harm reduction among staff. We provide here a sample agenda using much of the material on childhood sexuality in Chapter 6.

Camp ABC Policy on Staff / Camper Contact

Camp ABC must investigate every suspicion of child abuse, including sexual abuse.

If a staff member appears to have in any way abused a camper, the camp director will meet with the camper to gather details of the incident(s) focusing specifically on: who committed the act(s); when the act(s) occurred; where the act(s) occurred; what actually happened.

The director will contact the local authorities (police department or child protection agency) and allow their team to proceed with an investigation.

Parents of the involved child will be contacted following the investigation.

The police will meet with the accused. If the police believe that abuse has occurred, they will likely take the accused into custody.

It is this camp's policy to suspend individuals accused of child abuse. We rely on the criminal justice system to determine whether abuse has occurred. If the accusation is determined to be false, it will not be held against the individual in future hiring decisions.

	Camper Harm-Reduction Training
	Present examples of normative sexual behaviors for children. Discuss the camp's philosophy on normative sexual behaviors.
	Discuss problematic sexual behaviors. • Sexually intrusive behaviors • Compulsive and aggressive sexual behaviors
	Discuss and role-play proper responses to camper displays of sexual activity. Provide examples of appropriate and inappropriate verbal responses to discovered activity.
	Present samples of letters to parents (if used). • Safety letter • Unwelcome touch letter
	Present camper unwelcome behavior policy.
	Present camp response to reported staff/camper contact. • Policy on child abuse allegations • Necessity of investigation by local authorities
	Discuss monitoring protocol for above polices. Discuss role of staff in monitoring each other's behavior.
	Time for questions and answers.

Proactive Monitoring of Harmful Behavior

I do not want to leave you with the misconception that creating policies against unwanted sexual activity will stop all instances. If having a policy were enough to stop a behavior, we should have seen a distinct drop in sexual harassment in the workplace over the last decade as more employers adopted sexual harassment policies. This has not happened. Directors need to be proactive to cut down on inappropriate activity.

The case of alcohol use provides a good example. Most camps have a policy forbidding alcohol use, but only with the advent of cost-efficient, easy-to-use, valid testing equipment have camps been able to put "teeth" into the policy. We are in need of similar "teeth" for our policies on harmful sexual activity. Knowing that most cases of inappropriate sexual activity are never voluntarily reported, and that few staff avail themselves of a camp director's "open door" policy to discuss problematic sexual behaviors, how can we truly make a difference in reducing harmful sexual activity in camps? How do we prove to parents that we spare no effort to protect their children?

For now, the best we can offer is highly proactive monitoring. This goes well beyond the standard practice of "management by walking around." Directors already know that campers should not be left unsupervised, especially in showers and when changing clothing. Staff should never be alone with campers, should not roughhouse with campers, and should not offer massages or back rubs. Camp administrators can be on the lookout for these activities. What we need to address are those unwelcome sexual behaviors that are hidden from our view. Even the most rigorous scrutiny will not turn up the vast majority of these incidents. But a director can be sensitive to signs of troubling undercurrents. A seemingly isolated report of unwanted physical contact should send up a red flag that there may be problems with the general environment of the camp. Maybe it is less safe than the director thought.

One way to address the limitations of walk-around monitoring is to seek feedback from all camp participants. Implementing a program of regular formal and informal surveys is the closest thing we have to putting "teeth" in our policies.

We end this book with two surveys designed to evaluate your camp's safety plan—one for staff and one for campers. The surveys are not geared solely to inappropriate sexual activity, although a director could modify them for this purpose. Rather, they evaluate a range of factors that affect the camp environment, especially those aspects of camp culture highlighted in Chapter 3.

My rationale for proposing a more general safety survey instead of one that is sex-specific is simply that *any* negative influence in camp may lead to inappropriate sexual activity. Recall that child molesters seek out specific environments that lend themselves to the sexual abuse of children. A survey focused on sexual activity would likely catch such activity only after the fact. **By focusing on the general environment of the camp, we have a better chance of intervening and making positive changes before a serious incident occurs.** Our purpose with these surveys is to do both: determine whether inappropriate sexual activity has already occurred, and learn of environmental factors that could foster such activity.

Surveying Staff

The following staff survey can be completed in ten minutes or so. It is anonymous, though staff can certainly give their names if they want to. The staff should clearly be told the purpose of the survey: to help the administration detect harmful influences in camp and to assist in implementing a general safety plan.

To stress its importance, the director him- or herself should introduce the survey. The director should present the survey as an important tool for all camp staff and emphasize that the administration is available to discuss any and all safety concerns. Completion of the survey should not be rushed or appear as an afterthought to an already packed meeting agenda.

Timing of the survey is important. Administering the survey during staff week may not give enough time for harmful camp influences to make themselves known. Administering it at the conclusion of the season leaves no time for implementing positive change. Thus I recommend administering the survey at least twice during the season. The first survey can be used as a baseline audit for possible problems and can lead to changes in camp protocols and policies. The second survey can provide evidence of whether the changes have been successful.

No special science is needed to interpret the survey results—they will either match or contradict the camp administration's general impression. Use the results as a starting point for modifying the camp safety plan and for gathering more information. It is only fair to inform staff of the survey findings. This is also the ideal time to present changes that camp administration will implement to positively affect camp safety based on the survey. Some changes may include:

- Policy changes
- Formation of a committee to further address the findings
- Additional training
- Commitment of additional resources to camp safety

Staff Safety Survey

What is your gender?   ❑ Female   ❑ Male

Please give us your opinions on the following questions. Using the following scale, circle the number that most closely matches your opinion:

1 = strongly disagree
2 = disagree
3 = neutral
4 = agree
5 = strongly agree

1. This camp offers a safe experience for staff.   1 2 3 4 5

2. This camp offers a safe experience for campers.   1 2 3 4 5

3. The camp has a code of conduct that staff members are expected to follow.   1 2 3 4 5

4. Staff members are observed to assure that rules are followed.   1 2 3 4 5

5. Individuals with different backgrounds (gender, race, sexual orientation, international, etc.) are respected here.   1 2 3 4 5

6. At camp, do you think you have been a victim of any of the following? *Check all that apply.*

❑ Harassment   ❑ Discrimination   ❑ Bullying

7. Have you personally experienced any of the following in camp? *Check all that apply.*

❑ Leering

❑ Wolf whistles

❑ Discussion of another's sexual attributes and/or inadequacies

❑ Sexual innuendo

❑ Lewd and/or threatening letters

❑ Displays of pornography

❑ Another person exposed him- or herself to you

❑ Pressure for dates or sexual activity

❑ Sexually explicit gestures

❑ Unwelcome touching and hugging

❑ Sabotaging another person's work

❑ Sexist and insulting graffiti

❑ Inappropriate invitations

❑ Hostile put-downs

❑ Public humiliation

❑ Mockery

❑ Disrespectful treatment

❑ Assault and other unwanted physical contact

❑ Intimidation

❑ Threats

❑ Cruel or inappropriate practical jokes

❑ Destruction of personal property

8. Is the camp administration approachable if problems arise?   ❑ Yes   ❑ No

In your opinion, how could the administration become more approachable?

9. Do you personally feel safe in this camp?   ❑ Yes   ❑ No

If not, what could be done to increase your security?

Please use this space to address any additional concerns you may have.

Surveying Campers

Many camps implement a survey informally by having administrative staff sit at random tables with campers at lunchtime and ask safety-oriented questions. By the end of the encampment, most campers will have had a chance to share a meal with someone from the administration. It was just this method that detected the staff member who took his cabin for a nude swim.

A more formal means of surveying campers is to have someone from the administration or nursing staff visit each unit group and ask questions or administer a written evaluation. Unit staff are asked to leave for the duration of the survey. Units do not need to be surveyed all at the same time.

In such informal and formal conversations, campers often willingly give administration feedback about their camp experience. All feedback is valuable, but we are especially seeking safety-oriented feedback. Although it may be tempting to ask children direct questions—"Has anybody touched your genitals at camp?"—such an approach is too intimidating for many children. A supplementary written survey overcomes the limitations of direct questioning. We offer a sample written survey as a guideline. **Staff should be shown the camper survey during staff orientation week.** This alerts staff to the administration's seriousness and determination to prevent inappropriate behaviors.

Select an appropriate individual to administer the written survey as follows:

1. Read aloud the camp "unwelcome behavior" policy as presented in the harm-reduction agenda for campers on page 139. This should not be the first time the campers have heard the policy.

2. Explain that the purpose of the survey is to help the camp administration keep campers safe.

3. Hand out the survey and go over the questions. For question 5 on the survey, ask campers to write the letter "S" for staff or "C" for camper next to the checked behaviors if they want to say who actually committed the acts.

4. Give the campers ample time to complete the survey. Tell them that when they complete the survey, they may return to their cabins. Also say that you will wait around for awhile after the last survey is completed to talk privately to interested campers. (Such a private meeting could be the one time that an episode of sexually inappropriate behavior is revealed.)

5. Remind campers that a specific staff member is available to discuss safety concerns at any time.

Camper Safety Survey

This survey was completed by a ❑ Female ❑ Male

Your name (optional) _____

Name of your unit/group_____

1. Do you feel safe in this camp? ❑ Yes ❑ No ❑ Not sure

2. Has anybody made you uncomfortable in camp? ❑ Yes ❑ No ❑ Not sure

3. Who was the person who made you feel uncomfortable?

   ❑ A camper   ❑ A staff member   ❑ I have not been uncomfortable

4. What did this person do that made you feel uncomfortable?

_____

_____

_____

5. Check any of the following that *have happened to you at camp* OR that *you have seen happen to another camper*. You may mark the behavior with a letter to show that it was done by a camper (C) or staff member (S).

   ❑ Was scared by another person

   ❑ Was threatened by another person

   ❑ Had a cruel practical joke played on them

   ❑ Had personal property destroyed

   ❑ Had their body talked about

   ❑ Saw pornography

   ❑ Was pressured for dates or sexual activity

   ❑ Was made uncomfortable by touching or hugging

6. Has a staff member asked you to help keep secrets? ❑ Yes ❑ No

7. Write down one thing that would make you feel more comfortable in camp.

_____

_____

_____

_____

Appendix

Surveys	Page
Mom and Dad Said	148
Values, Attitudes, and Feelings Regarding Sex and Sexuality (A) Questionnaire	150
Analyzing Our Values, Attitudes, and Feelings Regarding Sex and Sexuality (A) Work Sheet	152
Adults' Sexual Behaviors as Children	153
Adults' Sexual Behaviors as Children—Sample Responses	155
Family Roles, Relationships, Behaviors, and Practices I	158

Letters to Parents	Page
Sample Safety Letter	163
Sample Unwelcome Touch Letter	165
Teaching Children About Their Private Parts	166

Mom and Dad Said

Below are questions regarding sex and sexuality. Complete the sentences and then circle (A) if you agree or (D) if you disagree. Your parents may not have actually stated their opinion on the topic. You may have picked up their opinion from their actions or other things they said.

About Masturbation

Mom said _____ A   D

Dad said _____ A   D

About Contraception

Mom said _____ A   D

Dad said _____ A   D

About Love

Mom said _____ A   D

Dad said _____ A   D

About Sexual Intercourse

Mom said _____ A   D

Dad said _____ A   D

About Men

Mom said _____ A   D

Dad said _____ A   D

About Women

Mom said _____ A   D

Dad said _____ A   D

About Marriage

Mom said _____ A   D

Dad said _____ A   D

About Homosexuality

Mom said _____ A   D

Dad said _____ A   D

About Abortion

Mom said _____   A   D

Dad said _____   A   D

About Age for First Sexual Experience

Mom said _____   A   D

Dad said _____   A   D

About Extramarital Sexual Relations

Mom said _____   A   D

Dad said _____   A   D

Was your mother's behavior about extramarital sex the same as she taught you it should be?

❑ Yes   ❑ No   Don't know _____

Was your father's behavior about extramarital sex the same as he taught you it should be?

❑ Yes   ❑ No   Don't know _____

Values, Attitudes, and Feelings
Regarding Sex and Sexuality (A) Questionnaire

Following is a list of statements. Please rate each item on a 1 to 5 scale according to how true or untrue the statement is about you and your beliefs.

Circle: 1 = True, 2 = Sort of true, 3 = Don't know, 4 = Sort of false, 5 = False.

1.	Sexual relationships provide an important and fulfilling part of my life.	1	2	3	4	5
2.	It is all right to *ask* for sex from a partner.	1	2	3	4	5
3.	Sex between adults and children is sometimes okay.	1	2	3	4	5
4.	Sex is "dirty."	1	2	3	4	5
5.	Children should be told about contraceptives as soon as they start to be sexually active.	1	2	3	4	5
6.	Sexually, I feel like a failure.	1	2	3	4	5
7.	Masturbation by *adults* is acceptable in private.	1	2	3	4	5
8.	Masturbation by a *child* is acceptable in private.	1	2	3	4	5
9.	Adults should be able to view pornography if they choose.	1	2	3	4	5
10.	A woman should always be available sexually to her lover.	1	2	3	4	5
11.	I have told the "facts of life" to my child.	1	2	3	4	5
12.	Overall, I am satisfied with my sex life.	1	2	3	4	5
13.	A sexual relationship should include more than sexual intercourse.	1	2	3	4	5
14.	There are sexual practices between consenting adults that are wrong under any circumstances. If you agree, give some examples. _____ _____	1	2	3	4	5
15.	Adult nudity in the home is okay, even with children present.	1	2	3	4	5
16.	A man should always be available sexually to his lover.	1	2	3	4	5
17.	I have sexual feelings I do not understand.	1	2	3	4	5

©Toni Cavanagh Johnson, Ph.D., 1101 Fremont Ave., South Pasadena, CA 91030. Reprinted with permission.

18.	Sexual relationships create more problems than they're worth.	1	2	3	4	5
19.	The use of contraceptives is very important.	1	2	3	4	5
20.	I have trouble knowing what my beliefs and values are regarding my sexual behavior.	1	2	3	4	5
21.	My child is like I was sexually when I was a child.	1	2	3	4	5
22.	I am more sexual than other people of the same sex.	1	2	3	4	5
23.	I daydream about sex.	1	2	3	4	5
24.	When I'm in a sexual situation, I get confused about my feelings.	1	2	3	4	5
25.	I have respect for the way I act sexually.	1	2	3	4	5
26.	Homosexuality is wrong.	1	2	3	4	5
27.	Married partners have the right to say "no" to sex with their spouse.	1	2	3	4	5
28.	I sometimes make bad decisions about my sexual behavior.	1	2	3	4	5
29.	I sometimes blame someone else for my sexual behavior.	1	2	3	4	5
30.	I sometimes do sexual things without worrying about the consequences.	1	2	3	4	5
31.	In general, I like my body.	1	2	3	4	5
32.	Casual sex is okay.	1	2	3	4	5
33.	The way parents act is a great influence on their child's sexual attitudes and behaviors.	1	2	3	4	5
34.	I want my child to have the same values about sex as I do.	1	2	3	4	5
35.	My child knows my values and attitudes regarding sex.	1	2	3	4	5
36.	When I have problems in my adult relationships, I discuss them with my child.	1	2	3	4	5
37.	I worry about my child being sexual with others.	1	2	3	4	5
38.	It is all right for two people to have sex before marriage.	1	2	3	4	5

Analyzing Our Values, Attitudes, and Feelings Regarding Sex and Sexuality (A) Work Sheet

Please answer the following questions regarding various areas of sexuality.

At approximately what age is it all right to begin to have sexual contact (kissing, touching, petting) with another person?

Is masturbation okay? If your answer is yes, when is it okay? If your answer is no, why is masturbation not okay? If your answer is sometimes, when is masturbation all right, by whom and under what circumstances?

Is the use of contraceptives okay? When should contraceptives be used? Who should use contraceptives? At what age should people get information about contraceptives?

How should children learn about sex and sexuality?

Are you proud to be a member of your sex? If so, why? If not, why not? How does this affect the way you act?

After two people have met, what decision process do, or should, two people go through when deciding to have sexual relations with one another?

Is abortion an acceptable method of birth control?

What are your feelings about heterosexuality? What are your feelings about homosexuality? What are your feelings about bisexuality?

What do you think about pornography? Should it be in the home?

Are there sexual practices that you do not find acceptable? For example, is oral sex an acceptable sexual practice?

Are there any forms of sexual expression between adults and children that are acceptable?

If two people are married, is it acceptable for them to have sexual relations outside of their marriage?

What should a man and woman think about *before* agreeing to have sexual relations that might result in pregnancy? Is it your experience that people think about these things?

Are there any things you do in the area of sex and sexuality that you would not want your parents to know?

Sometimes parents use their children to meet their own needs. For example, a parent may sleep with a child as a way to deal with their own needs for sexual closeness. Have you ever seen this happen?

Which of your attitudes and values regarding sex and sexuality are guided by your religious values?

Adults' Sexual Behaviors as Children

Name:_____ Male or Female:_____ Your Age:_____

Please check the behaviors you engaged in when you were twelve years or younger.

❑ Invitation or request to do something sexual

❑ Teasing at school by running/peaking in bathroom, lifting skirts, telling dirty jokes

❑ Playing "doctor"

❑ Talking about sex

❑ Kissing or hugging other child

❑ Showing "private parts" to other child

❑ Touching, exploring, masturbation of self

❑ Touching, exploring "private parts" of other child

❑ Looking at "dirty pictures"

❑ Watching people in bathroom, bedroom, etc., when they are unaware of child's presence

❑ Putting objects in the vagina or rectum of another child

❑ Putting mouth on penis or vagina of another child

❑ "Humping" or pretending intercourse

❑ Vaginal intercourse

❑ Anal intercourse

❑ Sexual contact with animal(s)

❑ Putting objects in own vagina/rectum

❑ Other _____

While you were engaging in the sexual behaviors between six and ten years old and eleven and twelve years old, how did you feel? Check (✔) as many as apply.

Feeling	Six to Ten Years	Eleven to Twelve Years
Good/fine		
Silly/giggly		
Excited (not sexually)		
Mad		
Bad		

©Toni Cavanagh Johnson, Ph.D., 1101 Fremont Ave., South Pasadena, CA 91030. Reprinted with permission.

Feeling	Six to Ten Years	Eleven to Twelve Years
Sexually stimulated (as an adult might feel)		
Pleasant body sensations		
Unpleasant body sensations		
Didn't like it		
Scared		
Guilty		
Confused		
Other: _____ _____		

Use the scale: 1 = No knowledge, 2 = Incorrect understanding, 3 = Some accurate knowledge, 4 = Accurate and complete understanding. How accurate do you think your understanding was of each of the following when you were twelve and younger?

_____ Conception

_____ Contraception

_____ Venereal diseases

_____ Sexual intercourse

_____ Abortion

_____ Masturbation

Did a parent(s) sit down with you to tell you "the facts of life"?

❑ Yes   ❑ No

How do you feel about your sexual experiences as a child?

❑ Bad   ❑ Sort of bad   ❑ Okay   ❑ Pretty good   ❑ Very good

Circle Yes or No. As a child were you?

Yes   No   Emotionally abused

Yes   No   Sexually abused

Yes   No   Observed violence in your family

Yes   No   Physically abused

Yes   No   Emotionally or physically neglected

Adults' Sexual Behaviors as Children—Sample Responses

The answers represent the responses of 352 mental health and child welfare workers who attended lectures by Toni Cavanagh Johnson, Ph.D., on the topic of children with sexual behavior problems in 1996–1997 in the United States.

Profession: Mental Health and Child Welfare—**352**
Male: **19%**   Female: **81%**
Age: Mean = **39**, Range = **18–72**

Please check the behaviors you engaged in when you were twelve years or younger.

34   Invitation or request to do something sexual

34   Teasing at school by running/peaking in bathroom, lifting skirts, telling dirty jokes

46   Playing "doctor"

53   Talking about sex

49   Kissing or hugging other child

30   Showing "private parts" to other child

47   Touching, exploring, masturbation of self

19   Touching, exploring "private parts" of other child

36   Looking at "dirty pictures"

9   Watching people in bathroom, bedroom, etc., when they are unaware of child's presence

3   Putting objects in the vagina or rectum of another child

2   Putting mouth on penis or vagina of another child

12   "Humping" or pretending intercourse

3   Vaginal intercourse

1   Anal intercourse

2   Sexual contact with animal(s)

5   Putting objects in own vagina/rectum

___   Other _____

While you were engaging in the sexual behaviors between six and ten years old and eleven and twelve years old, how did you feel? Check (✓) as many as apply.

Feeling	Six to Ten Years	Eleven to Twelve Years
Good/fine	29	27
Silly/giggly	44	28
Excited (not sexually)	21	18
Mad	4	3
Bad	15	11
Sexually stimulated (as an adult might feel)	9	21
Pleasant body sensations	27	32
Unpleasant body sensations	8	6
Didn't like it	11	7
Scared	21	17
Guilty	29	33
Confused	25	25

Other: _____

Use the scale: 1 = No knowledge, 2 = Incorrect understanding, 3 = Some accurate knowledge, 4 = Accurate and complete understanding. How accurate do you think your understanding was of each of the following when you were twelve and younger?

24 Conception

16 Contraception

14 Venereal diseases

24 Sexual intercourse

16 Abortion

19 Masturbation

Did a parent(s) sit down with you to tell you "the facts of life"?

33 Yes   **67** No

How do you feel about your sexual experiences as a child?

10 Bad   **19** Sort of bad   **48** Okay   **17** Pretty good   **6** Very good

Circle Yes or No. As a child were you?

Yes No   Emotionally abused   **27**

Yes No   Sexually abused   **22**

Yes No   Observed violence in your family   **28**

Yes No   Physically abused   **15**

Yes No   Emotionally or physically neglected   **24**

Family Roles, Relationships, Behaviors, and Practices I

Name:_____ Date:_____

Please go over the following statements and check those that remind you to some extent of:

Your family when you were growing up (on the left side of the page)

Your family now (on the right side of the page)

Parent–Child Relationships

❑	Sometimes the child acts as if he or she is the "parent." May take care of other children.	❑
❑	Child acts like a good friend or buddy of the parent, shares secrets and tries to take care of and make the parent feel better.	❑
❑	Child may be used as a substitute for a boyfriend/girlfriend or a partner.	❑
❑	Child pulled into the arguments of the parents.	❑
❑	Parents fight about sex in front of children.	❑
❑	Children allowed to listen to adult conversations about sex or sexuality.	❑
❑	Sexual problems of parents discussed around children.	❑
❑	Children know details of parents' sex lives.	❑

Relationships with People Outside the Family

❑	Family members' personal business told to people who do not need to know.	❑
❑	Personal questions asked of strangers.	❑
❑	People become "good" friends too easily.	❑
❑	Family has few friends. "Outsiders" kept out. Secrecy about what goes on in the family.	❑
❑	Strangers are asked to help out with family problems.	❑
❑	Unfamiliar people invited into the home. They are allowed to use anything they want.	❑

©Toni Cavanagh Johnson, Ph.D., 1101 Fremont Ave., South Pasadena, CA 91030. Reprinted with permission.

	Personal Privacy	
❏	No one's possessions are private and personal.	❏
❏	Family members meddle in others' "business" (i.e., plans, conversations, activities, relationships).	❏
❏	Family members sneak to look at others' things (i.e., diary, mail, or listen to telephone conversations).	❏
❏	Information told "in private" is shared with others (i.e., siblings, parents, relatives, neighbors, unfamiliar people).	❏
❏	Children are not allowed any personal belongings (i.e., toys that others can't use).	❏
	Personal Rights	
❏	Family members try to control others' behaviors (i.e., plans, conversations, activities, relationships, etc.).	❏
❏	Family members try to control others' thoughts, feelings, self-perceptions. "You'll never be any good," "Children must love their parents."	❏
❏	Children treated like possessions, slaves.	❏
❏	Parent ignores child's requests to sleep, bathe, dress alone.	❏
❏	Details of teenager's dates demanded.	❏
	Personal Feelings	
❏	Family members think they know how others are feeling, even when they don't. "You are just mad (sad, sick)."	❏
❏	Family members think others feel exactly the way they do, even when they don't. "We are so happy to be here together."	❏
❏	Family members confuse one person's feeling or actions with those of another. "You are mean to me just like your father (sister, etc.)."	❏
❏	Family members think of their own needs and forget about others'. "Call me from your job, forget about what your boss says." "You can do that later, I want you to do this for me now."	❏

	Shaming	
☐	Children's bodies are made fun of.	☐
☐	Children are made fun of for age-appropriate sexual curiosity.	☐
	Home Atmosphere	
☐	People don't keep their word (i.e., allowance, promises, privileges, gifts, picking up on time, stopping hurtful behavior, etc.).	☐
☐	Family members get out of control:	☐

☐	Drinking	☐
☐	Fighting	☐
☐	Gambling	☐
☐	Yelling	☐
☐	Drugs	☐
☐	Eating	☐
☐	Other? _____	☐

☐	Passing gas and burping considered amusing.	☐
☐	Rules for children not clear. They change frequently.	☐
	Bathroom Practices	
☐	No locks on bathroom doors.	☐
☐	Little or no privacy in the bathroom.	☐
☐	No doors on bathrooms/bedrooms (not due to poverty).	☐
☐	Parent bathes with school-aged child.	☐
☐	Holes in the bathroom or bedroom walls or doors (not due to poverty).	☐
☐	Family members invited into the bathroom while others use toilet.	☐
☐	Bathroom doors left open when people use the toilet, bath, shower.	☐

	Body Privacy	
❑	Children's body development talked about making child uncomfortable.	❑
❑	Children bathed/groomed after they are old enough to do it alone.	❑
❑	Kiss children on the mouth after eight years old.	❑
❑	Enemas, suppositories used for children when not necessary.	❑
❑	Children's genitals cleaned after they are old enough to do it alone.	❑
❑	Medicine applied to private areas of children's bodies after they are old enough to do it alone.	❑
❑	Unnecessary (unwanted) rubbing or touching of parts of another's body.	❑
❑	Children's growth and "private parts" are closely monitored by looking, touching, or constant questions about the children's body.	❑
❑	Children's genitals, breasts, bottom fondled or rubbed.	❑
❑	Insertion of things into children's genitals.	❑
	Personal Space Invasion	
❑	Physical space invaded (i.e., people stand/sit too close, get in their bed, read over shoulder, etc.).	❑
❑	Personal belongings (i.e., purse, brief case, bedroom, desk drawers, etc.) are gone into without asking.	❑
❑	Family members watch or peek at others without their knowledge.	❑
❑	Family members don't knock before opening doors of occupied rooms.	❑
❑	Children made to kiss or hug people they don't want to (i.e., strangers, relatives, siblings, parents).	❑
	Sexual Atmosphere	
❑	Sexually explicit and/or pornographic material left around the house.	❑
❑	X-rated or pornographic movies watched with children around.	❑
❑	Dirty language and jokes without regard to the children being around.	❑

❑	Sexual intercourse in front of children (not due to poverty and/or lack of private living space).	❑
❑	Sexual sounds during intercourse when child is awake and can hear them.	❑
❑	Nudity in front of children that makes them uncomfortable.	❑
❑	Sexual behavior while child in same bed "asleep."	❑
❑	Sexual mannerisms when children around (flirting, "dirty dancing," giving phone number to stranger).	❑
❑	Sexual comments made freely: "Look at those ta'taas." "I'd never throw him out of my bed." "Now there's a really fine butt."	❑
❑	Sexual behavior in front of children that makes them feel uncomfortable.	❑
❑	Children allowed/encouraged to touch genitals/breasts of others (when not by accident).	❑
❑	Family members' bodies used to show child "private parts" and explain "facts of life."	❑
❑	Sexual comments and behaviors between family members not consistently discouraged. Jokes may be made. "Look at your sister's chi-chi's. I bet you'd like to roll in the hay with her."	❑
❑	Sexual comments by children not consistently discouraged. "I like her boobies." "I'd like a piece of her ass."	❑
❑	Children encouraged to be nude or scantily dressed for adult's sexual interest.	❑
❑	Children encouraged to act in sexual (seductive) ways (i.e., walk, dress, language, sexual sounds, behaviors, mannerisms).	❑
❑	Pictures or movies taken of children in sexual poses, either nude or clothed.	❑

Sample Safety Letter

To: Parents and Guardians of Camp ABC Youngsters
From: The Smith Family—Owners/Directors
Date: September 2004
Re: A Safe Summer of 2005

Camp ABC has been successfully providing a summer of safe, age-appropriate, and memorable experiences for children for the last forty years. We have been pleased to be able to serve generations of families as well as multiple siblings from the same family. With few exceptions, Camp ABC has been able to serve all the children accepted for our program, and year after year parental praise for our work has been the rule. The Smith Family is grateful for all of your letters of appreciation and expressions of satisfaction with our efforts. We have every intention of continuing to care for your children with the same concern, interest, and energy in the 21st Century.

The success of our program is based, in part, on:

- High standards of care for your children.
- High expectations of ourselves and our staff.
- A value system explained to staff, campers, and families.
- Boundaries clearly defined for campers and staff.

Camp ABC is a community and a family. The well-being of your children both physically and emotionally is our priority. For us to continue to be successful, we need to make you aware of the observations and experiences we have been dealing with during the last four years. We believe that many children have been negatively influenced by song lyrics, sexually erotic television programming, movies, books, computer games, the Internet, and pornography. Our society appears to be focused on sexuality and violence, both of which idealize the use of drugs and alcohol. Our young people cannot avoid seeing, hearing, and absorbing that which makes up a substantial part of their lives. Our camp community is a microcosm of society at large. However, what may unfortunately be acceptable in some homes and communities cannot be acceptable in our Camp ABC Community if we are to continue to care for other people's children with the same concern, interest, and commitment to safety as we have in the past.

Our camp attempts to teach campers:

- To recognize that they have responsibility for themselves and those around them.
- To learn to make choices that are good for themselves and others, and to take responsibility for the choices they make.
- To respect oneself and others in spite of differences.
- To accept that they are accountable for their actions and the consequences for inappropriate behaviors.

It is essential that you communicate to your children that we will not be able to accept behaviors such as violence, possession of weapons, repeated profanity, disrespect, bigotry, inappropriate sexual behavior, drug and alcohol use, or any other unsafe behaviors that are potentially harmful to themselves or others. They must understand that a consequence of their behavior can mean the loss of this program.

Our demonstrated interest is to offer only pleasant memories. It is not our intent to exclude any child. However, that need may unfortunately arise. It is important to discuss in detail your expectations of your child(ren) and that we, parents and camp management, are in total agreement.

Another area of concern has been our experience with some children who have been sent to camp with "family secrets." Specifically, the children have fit some of these categories:

- Campers with psychiatric problems.
- Campers with serious medical problems.
- Campers with organic problems who are off medication for the summer.
- Campers who were hospitalized for physical or emotional reasons since last summer.
- Campers experiencing a traumatic reaction to family issues such as parental separation, divorce, or death.

In fairness to our counselors, staff, and campers, we need to make informed decisions about all of the young people we invite into our community and family. "Family secrets" serve no one. Our purpose in having pertinent health information, both physical and emotional, is to be able to better serve each child. We must expect parents or guardians of any child sent to Camp ABC to provide us with all the necessary information we need to keep all children safe.

With these facts in mind, as owner/directors of Camp ABC, we reserve the right to ask that a child at risk to oneself or the community be picked up and removed immediately from camp. There may be a circumstance where we have agreed to accept a child with full knowledge of his or her problems and have attempted to take all necessary steps to make the experience successful, but find that we are unable to do so. For the good of this child and/or the community, the child may have to leave.

This letter would have been unheard of fifteen years ago. However, the world has changed and we need to accept the effects of some of those changes. Please sign this letter and return it with your application materials for 2005. As always, please contact us if you have any questions or concerns about this communication or any other matter. We look forward to summer 2005.

Date: _____

Name of Parent(s) or Guardian(s) (please print): _____

_____

Signature(s) of Parent(s) or Guardian(s): _____

_____

Norman E. Friedman and William Young • AMSkier • 209 Main Avenue, Hawley PA 18428 • 800-245-2666
fax 570.226.1105 • e-mail amskier@aol.com • www.amskier.com

Sample Unwelcome Touch Letter

To: Parents and Guardians of Camp ABC Youngsters
From: The Smith Family—Owners/Directors
Date: September 2004
Re: Safety Materials to Share with Your Child

While summer 2004 is a vivid memory, those of us in leadership roles at camp are actively involved in evaluating this past summer as we carefully plan for summer 2005. When your children began school in September, so did we. Our "classroom" is made up of American Camping Association conferences both nationally and regionally. In addition, we attend special focus groups that help us study some interesting data to be learned from camps throughout the United States. Children nationwide who attended residential and day camps this past summer numbered close to ten million. We consider it an awesome responsibility to care for your most precious possessions. To that end, we accept the responsibility of learning as much as possible about ongoing or developing trends as well as new information to better fulfill our role as caregivers.

We take pride in our ability to carefully select the counselors and staff who work at ABC Camp. The selection process includes reference checks, professional recommendations, criminal and background checks, and interviews. We have a very high return rate of staff each summer, and that insures one of the most important aspects of camping—the culture of safety. We believe that the compulsory training programs we offer staff during orientation, as well as during the entire season, are state-of-the-art. We subscribe to the statement, "Good better best—never let it rest—until the good is better and the better is best."

At the American Camping Association conference held in New York City in March, we attended an educational session designed for camp owner/directors and all staff employed at camps. The session was focused on education and prevention of physical and sexual abuse of children in all congregate care programs. The instructor of the course was Norman E. Friedman, Director, Safety Underwriters Department, AMSkier. He has encouraged us to send you his recommendation, which has received national attention, about the important parental responsibility to teach their children about prevention of sexual abuse. Mr. Friedman believes that the most effective combatants in the war against pedophilia are the children themselves.

Our staff receives extensive training about the issues of physical and sexual abuse of children. However, our concerns for your children extend to the "off season"; as you well know, the reports of child molestation have been a number one issue in America during the last year. We agree with Mr. Friedman's hypothesis that a child carefully trained can effectively protect him/herself from sexual abuse. Mr. Friedman's materials are self-explanatory.

We hope the materials included are helpful. Norman Friedman has offered to answer any of your questions. He can be reached at NormanF@amskier.com. We look forward to once again caring for your children during the summer of 2005.

Enclosure

Norman E. Friedman, Director, Safety Underwriters Department, AMSkier • 209 Main Avenue, Hawley PA 18428 • 800-245-2666 • fax 570.226.1105 • email amskier@aol.com • www.amskier.com

Teaching Children about Their Private Parts

The parts of the body between the waist and knees may be touched only by the child, his/her parent(s), or guardian(s). There are no exceptions!

Most authorities on human sexuality and child development, including the American Pediatrics Association, agree that the names of all parts of the body should be taught to children by the time they are eighteen months old. Specifically, one should not differentiate or leave out any parts of the body in the teaching process. The list that follows, separated by gender, is appropriate to use to teach the names of the parts of the body. The shaded and italicized section of the table defines *private parts*.

Male	Female
Head	Head
Eyes	Eyes
Nose	Nose
Mouth	Mouth
Chin	Chin
Neck	Neck
Chest	Chest*
Abdomen	Abdomen
Navel	Navel
Penis	*Labia*
Scrotum	*Vagina*
Buttocks	*Buttocks*
Anus	*Anus*
Thigh	*Thigh*
Knee	Knee
Ankle	Ankle
Feet	Feet

*Puberty for a female designates the chest as a private part.

At approximately five years of age, children need to learn about their private parts. They are now ready to learn that the area between their waist and knees is a "no-touch zone." They must stop anyone who attempts to touch this area by simply saying, "You are not allowed to touch me there." They must then tell their parents what happened.

Child molesters who learn that a child is "savvy" will keep away. They rarely stand up to a child who just says, "No." They do not want to get caught.

Children love games. Learning the parts of the body is a fun game. Once learned, reviewing private parts at the appropriate time is very meaningful to a child and begins the process of self-protection. The most effective combatants in the war against pedophilia are the children themselves.

©January 2000 by Norman E. Friedman, Director, Safety Underwriters Department, AMSkier

References

American Camping Association (1998). *Accreditation Standards for Camp Programs and Services.*

American Psychiatric Association (2000). *Diagnostic and statistical manual of mental disorders,* 4th ed.

Andersson, M. (1982). Female choice selects for extreme tail length in a widowbird. *Nature,* 299, 818–820.

Anonymous. (2003). Who protects our children? *The CampLine,* 1, 13–15.

Araji, S. (1997). *Sexually aggressive children.* California: Sage Publications.

Bauman, S. (2002). Types of juvenile sex offenders. *The Prevention Researcher,* 9, 11–13.

Beck, A.T. (1988). *Love is never enough.* New York: HarperPerennial.

Becker, J., & Hunter, J. (1997). Understanding and treating child and adolescent sexual offenders. In T. Ollendick & R. Prinz (Eds.), *Advances in clinical child psychology,* volume 19 (pp. 177–197). New York: Plenum Press.

Best, J. (2001). *Damned lies and statistics.* California: University of California Press.

Best, J., & Horiuchi, G. (1985). The blade in the apple. *Social Problems,* 32, 488–499.

Blackmore, S. (1999). *The meme machine.* New York: Oxford.

Blum, D. (1997). *Sex on the brain: The biological differences between men and women.* New York: Viking Press.

Bordo, S. (1999). *The male body.* New York: Farrar, Straus, & Giroux.

Bradley, S. (2003). Abstinence only: The policy that will increase teen pregnancy. *The Reporter,* 35, 16–21.

Braverman, M. (1999). *Preventing workplace violence: A guide for employers and practitioners.* California: Sage Publications.

Briere, J. (1992). *Child abuse trauma: Theory and treatment of the lasting effects.* California: Sage Publications.

Briere, J., & Runtz, M. (1989). University males' sexual interest in children: Predicting potential indices of "pedophilia" in a nonforensic sample. *Child Abuse and Neglect,* 1, 65–75.

Briggs, D., Doyle, P., Gooch, T., & Kennington, R. (1998). *Assessing men who sexually abuse.* Pennsylvania: Jessica Kingsley Publishers.

Buck, R. (2002). The genetics and biology of true love: Prosocial biological affects and the left hemisphere. *Psychological Review,* 109, 739–744.

Buerkel-Rothfuss, N. (1993). Background: What prior research shows. In B. Greenberg, J. Brown, & N. Buerkel-Rothfuss (Eds.), *Media, sex and the adolescent.* New York: Hampton Press.

Bukowski, W., Hoza, B., & Boivin, M. (1993). Popularity, friendship, and emotional adjustment during early adolescence. In B. Laursen (Ed.), *Close friendships in adolescence* (pp. 23–37). California: Jossey-Bass Publishers.

Bukowski, W., Sippola, L., & Brender, W. (1993). Where does sexuality come from? Normative sexuality from a developmental perspective. In H. Barbaree, W. Marshall, & S. Hudson (Eds.), *The juvenile sex offender* (pp. 84–103). New York: The Guilford Press.

Buss, D. (2003). *The evolution of desire.* New York: Basic Books.

Buss, D. (2000). *The dangerous passion.* New York: The Free Press.

Buss, D., Larsen, R., & Westen, D. (1996). Sex differences in jealousy: Not gone, not forgotten, and not explained by other hypotheses. *Psychological Science,* 7, 373–375.

Butts, J.A., & Snyder, H.N. (1997). The youngest delinquents: Offenders under age 15. *Juvenile Justice Bulletin,* 1–10.

Campbell, A., Converse, P., & Rodgers, W. (1976). *The quality of American life.* New York: Sage Publications.

Cavanagh Johnson, T. (1998). *Treatment exercises for child abuse victims and children with sexual behavior problems.*

Cavanagh Johnson, T. (1999). *Sexuality curriculum for abused children and young adolescents and their parents.*

Cavanagh Johnson, T. (1999). *Understanding your child's sexual behavior.* California: New Harbinger Publications.

Clark, R., & Hatfield, E. (1989). Gender differences in receptivity to sexual offers. *Journal of Psychology and Human Sexuality,* 2, 39–55.

Collins, W.A., Hennighausen, K., Schmit, D., & Sroufe, L.A. (1997). Developmental precursors of romantic relationships: A longitudinal perspective. In S. Shulman & W.A. Collins (Eds.), *Romantic relationships in adolescence: Developmental perspectives* (pp. 69–84). California: Jossey-Bass Publishers.

Crepault, C., & Coulture, M. (1980). Men's erotic fantasies. *Archives of Sexual Behavior,* 6, 565–581.

Csikszentmihalyi, M. (1999). If we are so rich, why aren't we happy? *American Psychologist,* 54, 821–827.

DeKeseredy, W., & Kelly, K. (1993). The incidence and prevalence of woman abuse in Canadian university and college dating relationships. *Canadian Journal of Sociology,* 18, 137–159.

Diener, E., Wolsic, B., & Fujita, F. (1995). Physical attractiveness and subjective well-being. *Journal of Personality and Social Psychology,* 69, 120–129.

Ditter, B. (2002). In the trenches: Sensitive issues. *Camping Magazine,* Nov/Dec, 13–14.

Ditter, B. (2003): In the trenches: Communication breakdowns. *Camping Magazine,* Jan/Feb, 58–59.

Ditter, B. (2003). In the trenches: Working with camper parents. *Camping Magazine,* May/June, 52–53.

Dorfman, L. (1997). Youth and violence on local television news in California. *American Journal of Public Health,* 87, 1311–1316.

Fabes, R. (1994). Physiological, emotional, and behavioral correlates of gender segregation. In C. Leaper (Ed.), *Childhood gender segregation: Causes and consequences* (pp.19–34). California: Jossey-Bass Publishers.

Fagan, P., Wise, T., Schmidt, C., & Berlin, F. (2002). Pedophilia. *Journal of the American Medical Association,* 19, 2458–2465.

Fagot, B. (1994). Peer relations and the development of competence in boys and girls. In C. Leaper (Ed.), *Childhood gender segregation: Causes and consequences* (pp.53–65). California: Jossey-Bass Publishers.

Felson, R.B. (2002). *Violence and gender reexamined.* Washington: American Psychological Association.

Finkelhor, D. and Associates. (1986). *A sourcebook on child sexual abuse.* California: Sage Publications.

Furman, W. (1993). Theory is not a four-letter word: Needed directions in the study of adolescent friendships. In B. Laursen (Ed.), *Close friendships in adolescence* (pp. 89–103). California: Jossey-Bass Publishers.

Furman, W. & Wehner, E. (1997). Adolescent romantic relationships: A developmental perspective. In S. Shulman & W.A. Collins (Eds.), *Romantic relationships in adolescence: Developmental perspectives* (pp. 21–36). California: Jossey-Bass Publishers.

Gabriel, Y., Fineman, S., & Sims, D. (2000). *Organizing and organizations*. California: Sage Publications.

Garbarino, J., & deLara, E. (2002). *And words can hurt forever*. New York: The Free Press.

Giacalone, R., & Greenberg, J. (1997). *Antisocial behavior in organizations*. California: Sage Publications.

Glassner, B. (1999). *The culture of fear*. New York: Basic Books.

Greer, A.E., & Buss, D. M. (1994). Tactics for promoting sexual encounters. *Journal of Sex Research,* 31, 185–201.

Griffeth, R., & Hom, P. (2001). *Retaining valued employees*. California: Sage Publications.

Grisso, T. (1998). *Forensic evaluation of juveniles*. Florida: Professional Resource Press.

Hamer, D., & Copeland, P. (1998). *Living with our genes*. New York: Doubleday.

Hartup, W. (1993). Adolescents and their friends. In B. Laursen (Ed.), *Close friendships in adolescence* (pp. 3–22). California: Jossey-Bass Publishers.

Hearn, J. & Parkin, W. (2001). *Gender, sexuality, and violence in organizations*. California: Sage Publications.

Hendrick, C., & Hendrick, S. (1989). Research on love: Does it measure up? *Journal of Personality and Social Psychology,* 56, 784–794.

Hussain, R., Schofield, M., & Loxton, D. (2002). Cosmetic surgery history and health service use in midlife: Women's health Australia. *Medical Journal of Australia,* 176, 576–579.

Karr-Morse, R., & Wiley, M. (1997). *Ghosts from the nursery*. New York: Atlantic Monthly Press.

Kennedy, D. (2002). Are there things we'd rather not know? *Cerebrum,* 3, 67–68.

Kennedy-Moore, E., & Watson, J. (1999). *Expressing emotion*. New York: Guilford.

Kiger, P., & Sorgen, C. (2000). A loss of innocents. *Good Housekeeping,* May, 118–121 & 184–189.

Kimura, D. (2000). A scientist dissents on sex and cognition. *Cerebrum,* 4, 68–84.

Koss, M.P., Gidycz, C.A., & Wisniewski, N. (1987). The scope of rape: Incidence and prevalence of sexual aggression and victimization in a national sample of students in higher education. *Journal of Consulting and Clinical Psychology,* 55, 162–170.

Kunkel, D. (1994). How the news media see kids. *Media Studies Journal,* 8, 74–84.

Langer, E.J. (1975). The illusion of control. *Journal of Personality and Social Psychology,* 32, 311–328.

Laursen, B. (1993). Conflict management among close peers. In B. Laursen (Ed.), *Close friendships in adolescence* (pp. 39–54). California: Jossey-Bass Publishers.

Laursen, B. & Williams, V. (1997). Perceptions of interdependence and closeness in family and peer relationships amongst adolescents with and without romantic partners. In S. Shulman & W.A. Collins (Eds.), *Romantic relationships in adolescence: Developmental perspectives* (pp 3–20). California: Jossey-Bass Publishers.

Leaper, C. (1994). Exploring the consequences of gender segregation on social relationships. In C. Leaper (Ed.), *Childhood gender segregation: Causes and consequences* (pp.67–86). California: Jossey-Bass Publishers.

Leaper, C., & Anderson, K. (1997). Gender development and heterosexual romantic relationships during adolescence. In S. Shulman & W.A. Collins (Eds.), *Romantic relationships in adolescence: Developmental perspectives* (pp. 85–103). California: Jossey-Bass Publishers.

Levesque, R.J.R. (2000). *Adolescents, sex, and the law: Preparing adolescents for responsible citizenship.* Washington: American Psychological Association.

Levine, J. (2002). *Harmful to minors.* Minnesota: University of Minnesota Press.

Lewis, T., Amini, F., & Lannon, R. (2000). *A general theory of love.* New York: Random House.

Longo, R., & Blanchard, G. (2002). Prevention of sexual offending among adolescents. *The Prevention Researcher, 4,* 5–8.

Lowry, D., & Towles, D.E., (1989). Prime time TV portrayals of sex, contraception, and venereal diseases. *Journalism Quarterly, 66,* 347–352.

Maccoby, E. (1994). Commentary: Gender segregation in childhood. In C. Leaper (Ed.), *Childhood gender segregation: Causes and consequences* (pp.87–97). California: Jossey-Bass Publishers.

Martin, C.L. (1994). Cognitive influences on the development and maintenance of gender segregation. In C. Leaper (Ed.), *Childhood gender segregation: Causes and consequences* (pp.35–51). California: Jossey-Bass Publishers.

Martinson, F.M. (1997). Sexual development in infancy and childhood. In G. Ryan & S. Lane (Eds.), *Juvenile sexual offending* (pp. 36–58). California: Jossey-Bass Publishers.

Mast, C.K. *Sex respect: Parent-teacher guide.* Illinois: Respect Inc.

Masters, W., Johnson, V., & Kolodny, R. (1992). *Human sexuality.* New York: HarperCollins.

Meyer, H. (1998). When cupid aims at the workplace. *Nation's Business,* July, 57–59.

Molidor, C., Tolman, R., & Kober, J. (2000). Gender and contextual factors in adolescent dating violence. *The Prevention Researcher, 7,* 1–4.

Murray, D., Schwartz, J., & Lichter, S.R. (2001). *It ain't necessarily so.* Maryland: Rowman & Littlefield.

Myers, D. (1992). *The pursuit of happiness.* New York: Avon Books.

Myers, D. (1999). Close relationships and quality of life. In D. Kahneman, E. Diener, & N. Schwarz (Eds.), *Well-being: The foundations of hedonic psychology* (pp. 374–391). New York: Russell Sage Foundation.

Myers, D. (2000). The funds, friends, and faith of happy people. *American Psychologist, 55,* 56–67.

Padavic, I., & Reskin, B. (2002). *Women and men at work.* California: Sage.

Perper, T., & Weis, D. (1987). Proceptive and rejective strategies of U.S. and Canadian college women. *Journal of Sex Research, 23,* 455–480.

Pinker, S. (1997). *How the mind works.* New York: Norton.

Pithers, W., & Gray, A. (1998). The other half of the story: Children with sexual behavior problems. *Psychology, Public Policy, and Law, 4,* 200–217.

Potts, M., & Short, R. (1999). *Ever since Adam and Eve.* New York: Cambridge University Press.

Ross, R. (1994). The ladder of inference. In P. Senge, R. Ross, B. Smith, C. Roberts, & A. Kleiner (Eds.), *The fifth discipline fieldbook.* New York: Currency Doubleday.

Rutter, P. (1996). *Sex, power, and boundaries.* New York: Bantam.

Sarwer, D., Wadden, T., Pertschuk, M., & Whitaker, L. (1998). The psychology of cosmetic surgery: A review and reconceptualization. *Clinical Psychology Review,* 18, 1–22.

Scanlin, M. (2002). Summary of 2002 ACA hotline calls. *The CampLine,* 2, 1 & 8–9.

Scanlin, M. (2003). Summary of ACA hotline calls. *The CampLine,* 2, 1 & 8–9.

Seiffge-Krenke, I. (1993). Close friendship and imaginary companions in adolescence. In B. Laursen (Ed.), *Close friendships in adolescence* (pp. 73–87). California: Jossey-Bass Publishers.

Seiffge-Krenke, I. (1997). The capacity to balance intimacy and conflict: Differences in romantic relationships between healthy and diabetic adolescents. In S. Shulman & W.A. Collins (Eds.), *Romantic relationships in adolescence: Developmental perspectives* (pp 53–67). California: Jossey-Bass Publishers.

Seligman, M.E. (2002). *Authentic happiness.* New York: Free Press.

Serbin, L., Moller, L., Gulko, J., Powlishta, K., & Colburne, K. (1994). The emergence of gender segregation in toddler playgroups. In C. Leaper (Ed.), *Childhood gender segregation: Causes and consequences* (pp 7–17). California: Jossey-Bass Publishers.

Shelton, M. (2003). *Coaching the camp coach.* Indiana: American Camping Association.

Shulman, S. (1993). Close friendships in early and middle adolescence: Typology and friendship reasoning. In B. Laursen (Ed.), *Close friendships in adolescence* (pp. 55–71). California: Jossey-Bass Publishers.

Shulman, S., Collins, W.A., & Knafo, D. (1997). Afterward: Romantic relationships in adolescence—more than casual dating. In S. Shulman & W.A.

Collins (Eds.), *Romantic relationships in adolescence: Developmental perspectives* (pp. 105–110). California: Jossey-Bass Publishers.

Shulman, S., Levy-Shiff, R., Kedem, P., & Alon, E. (1997). Intimate relationships among adolescent romantic partners and same-sex friends: Individual and systemic perspectives. In S. Shulman & W.A. Collins (Eds.), *Romantic relationships in adolescence: Developmental perspectives* (pp 37–51). California: Jossey-Bass Publishers.

Siegel, D.J. (1999). *The developing mind.* New York: The Guilford Press.

Stengers, J., & Van Neck, A. (2001). *Masturbation: The history of a great terror.* New York: St. Martin's Press.

Sternberg, R. (1986). A triangular theory of love. *Psychological Review,* 93, 119–135.

Steyer, J. (2002). The other parent. New York: Atria Books.

Tat, P., Cunningham, W., & Babakus, E. (1988). Consumer perceptions of rebates. *Journal of Advertising Research,* 28, 45–50.

Tissot, S. (1760). *L'Onanisme.*

Tobin, J. (1997). Playing doctor in two cultures. In J. Tobin (Ed.), *Making a place for pleasure in early childhood education* (pp. 119–158). Connecticut: Yale University Press.

Trivits, L., & Reppucci, N.D. (2002). Application of Megan's law to juveniles. *American Psychologist,* 57, 690–704.

van Dam, C. (2001). *Identifying child molesters.* New York: Haworth Maltreatment and Trauma Press.

Wagner, E. (1992). *Sexual harassment in the workplace.* New York: Amacom.

Warr, P. & Payne, R. (1982). Experience of strain and pleasure among British adults. *Social Science and Medicine,* 16, 498–516.

White, J., & Koss, M. (1992). Courtship violence: Incidence in a national sample of higher education students. *Violence and Victims, 6,* 247–256.

Wolfe, D., Wekerle, C., Reitzel-Jaffe, D., & Gough, R. (1995). Promoting healthy, nonviolent relationships among at-risk youth. In E. Peled, P. Jaffe, & J. Edelson (Eds.), *Ending the cycle of violence: Community responses to children of battered women* (pp. 255–274). California: Sage Publications.

Wolfe, D., Wekerle, C., & Scott, K. (1997). *Alternatives to violence: Empowering youth to develop healthy relationships.* California: Sage Publications.

Index